GET AWAY

How to take your youth group away – and survive

Arlo Reichter and others

BIBLE SOCIETY

IN ASSOCIATION WITH

BRITISH AND FOREIGN BIBLE SOCIETY
Stonehill Green, Westlea, SWINDON SN5 7DG, England

Unless otherwise stated, quotations from the Bible are from the
Good News Bible, published by the Bible Societies/Collins,
© American Bible Society, New York, 1966, 1971, 1976.

First published 1991

British Library Cataloguing in Publication Data
Reichter, Arlo
    Get away: how to take your youth group away – and survive.
    1. Adolescents, Vacations, Planning
    I. Title II. Reichter, Arlo. *Group retreat book* 259.23
    ISBN 0-564-05755-X

Printed in Great Britain by BPCC Wheatons Ltd, Exeter

Bible Societies exist to provide resources for Bible distribution and
use. Bible Society in England and Wales (BFBS) is a member of the
United Bible Societies, an international partnership working in over
180 countries. Their common aim is to reach all people with the
Bible, or some part of it, in a language they can understand and at a
price they can afford. Parts of the Bible have now been translated
into approximately 1900 languages. Bible Societies aim to help
every church at every point where it uses the Bible. You are invited
to share in this work by your prayers and gifts. Bible Society in
your country will be very happy to provide details of its activity.

Contents

		Page
Foreword *by Bob Moffett*		v
PART ONE	THE PLANNING GUIDE	
Chapter 1	Get started right: deciding purposes and goals	1
Chapter 2	How to plan a weekend away	4
Chapter 3	Choosing the best venue	10
Chapter 4	Getting there: tips for transporting your group	14
Chapter 5	Setting a budget that works	18
Chapter 6	Publicity and promotion: how to increase attendance at your weekend away	23
Chapter 7	Leaders and helpers	32
Chapter 8	Rules	36
Chapter 9	When you have a problem with someone	40
Chapter 10	Follow-up	45
Chapter 11	Planning checklists	48
Chapter 12	Two sample event programmes	51
Chapter 13	A selection of themes and formats	54
PART TWO	PROGRAMMES FOR YOUTH GROUP EVENTS	
Programme 1	Cliques	66
Programme 2	God's bod	81
Programme 3	Helping each other	93
Programme 4	Parents and teenagers	105
Programme 5	Blessed are the peacemakers	118
Programme 6	Experiencing blindness	126
Programme 7	Work camp	131
Programme 8	TV or not TV	135
Programme 9	An all-night lock-in	145
Selected reading list		150
Helpful organizations		151

Acknowledgements

The event programmes in the second half of this book were originally devised by:

Cindy Parolini, Virgil Nelson, Lynn Nelson *(Themes and formats)*

Kent Hummel *(Cliques)*

Jim Reeves, Tim Johnson, Deb Mechler *(God's bod)*

Bill Ameiss *(Helping each other)*

Wes Taylor *(Parents and teenagers)*

Edward McNulty *(Blessed are the peacemakers, TV or not TV)*

Joe Fowler *(Experiencing blindness)*

Tony Danhelka, Gary Richardson *(Work camp)*

Rickey Short *(An all-night lock-in)*

Foreword

by Bob Moffett

I really know when I like a "youth" book: it is when I'm envi-ous and jealous that he has written it before me and done a much better job than I ever could. Maybe that is not the best reason for writing a foreword but in this case I am pleased for a book of this quality and practicability to be on the market and bookshelves.

But this is the great thing about this book: it does not need to sit on the shelves to impress others that you take youth work seriously. This one is a down-to-earth "nuts and bolts" book of "how to". This is a book that can be taken by the novice leader and will help him or her prepare and action a creative event in safety and without too many frustrations. This book does not assume that you are a super dynamic, fantastic 99%, almost per-fect campaigner. In fact the old die-hard "we've always done it this way" survivors can learn a trick or thirty from this book.

A particularly useful part of this book is the themes. Anyone with a little nous knows that all Christian weekends should have three spiritual session "bits" a day, as I'm sure Moses encouraged in his forty-year camp! But it takes some initiative to run a whole day or weekend on a very creative theme or parable. Choosing a bride and groom through the Cinderella process, the bride's mother by which girl's head fits the enor-mous hat, are all ingredients for a glorious living parable of the Great Wedding Feast found in Matthew 22 or Luke 14.

Don't skimp on the first part of this book – it's a crucial preamble for the success of your event. Most events that fail are the ones that are poorly organized and are predictable in the first degree. Adapt the ideas to your young people but don't short-cut on the suggestions because of the lame excuse of "time". Young people are too valuable to God for you to let them down. This book is your Bible for youth weekends. Use it with a large spoonful of humour and a large dose of creativity sandwiched between two slices of prayer and practicalities and you could see many young lives changed – because you took your responsibilities seriously. So, thanks to Arlo Reichter, I'm set up for the next three or four years and you can bet that I won't credit the author publicly for his new insights and ideas other than here – you need to understand I'm just like every other youth worker!

PART ONE

THE PLANNING GUIDE

Chapter 1

Get started right: deciding purposes and goals

"We want to go swimming. That's what we came here for." My friend, the group leader, had a nasty problem on his hands. He'd planned the entire weekend by himself (and he was proud of it) for the purpose of helping the young people and their leaders grow in their faith. He assumed everyone else had the same purpose in mind, even though no one actually discussed purposes and goals with each other. Fortunately, everything worked out okay. After some on-the-spot planning the young people went swimming, and later many of the participants did grow in their faith because of the weekend.

My friend could have saved himself, and everyone else, needless tense moments by answering one very important question.

Why do we take youth groups away?

This is a question that's well worth your time as you consider your church's overall youth work. Reflect for a moment and then jot down your responses to it. Your group, their parents, and the church leadership should also ask themselves the question.

Worthy goals for weekends include fun, fellowship, recreation, Bible study, topical issues study, discipleship and faith growth. Any one weekend may include several of these goals or others which you find important. Whatever the goals, it is important for everyone who goes on a youth group weekend away to have the same goals in mind.

A general purpose statement for all such activities might be: "The purpose of time away is to set apart a time and place from the ordinary events of life during which a specific group of people can relate to one another in a variety of ways centred around a common theme."

Well in advance of any specific trip, meet with your church

leaders and develop a general purpose statement for it. Adapt the purpose statement suggested above so that it becomes a general statement for your church. After agreeing on a multi-purpose statement, discuss it with the youth group or a youth group representative.

Once the purpose statement is accepted, it's time to list possible goals such as:

- Building closer relationships
- Developing better understanding of God's Word
- In-depth study of issues faced by youth
- Study of a current social issue

Brainstorm a list of goals which your church's weekend might have. Involve young people and adults in this step. Everyone who agreed to the purpose statement should also be involved in the listing of possible goals.

Specific goals

Once a purpose statement and possible goals are agreed upon and a weekend away seems appropriate, the planning group for a specific event can determine which of the goals apply for that event. The planning group should also, of course, review the general purpose statement. The purpose statement and the various goals are guidelines and shouldn't be seen as unchangeable. Consider annual goal-setting sessions.

Goals for a specific weekend should be based on the particular needs of the youth group and the individual members of the group who will be a part of the activity they are planning.

It is helpful to plan the general flow of these experiences one year at a time, for example a weekend in autumn, winter, spring and summer. If this is the general flow of events, then a planning group might want to project tentative goals for each one. This is not to say that specific goals aren't important. But the year-long plan helps to cover a variety of needs during the year. It also adds variety to the events for the participants. General goals might be:

- Autumn: Building of relationships, getting to know new group members

- Winter: Developing a better understanding of God's Word, in-depth Bible study
- Spring: Understanding missions and other world issues
- Summer: In-depth study of personal issues

Of course, for many groups it may only be possible to plan one or two weekends away in a year, but this suggested flow of general goals could help to develop a constant growing and maturing of relationships between the participants. In turn, this allows them to share deeper and deeper personal issues and gain a more mature understanding and faith.

Youth programme components

Weekends away are only one part of your overall youth programme. Even though they are important, they are only one of several important components. To illustrate the parts of your youth programme try a simple diagram: draw a circle in the centre of a sheet of paper and write in it "our young people". Then draw several circles on the rest of the paper with arrows pointing towards this central circle. In these circles write the various components of your youth programme and draw lines connecting these different circles. This illustration of your church youth programme should accomplish three things:

1. Illustrate the various components of your youth programme.
2. Help you to realize that any one of the components cannot accomplish all you want to achieve in your youth programme.
3. Help you see how the different goals of each part can combine to make an effective ministry with young people.

Be realistic about taking groups away

A word of caution before we move on to the planning process for a specific event. *Be realistic with the goals you set.* Any one weekend is limited in what it can accomplish. Focus on a few goals for an activity and meet some of them. Focus on a large number of goals and end up frustrated by not having accomplished any.

Chapter 2

How to plan a weekend away

Planning process checklist

- Establish purpose and goals
- Select planning group
- Programme content and style
- Obtain leaders
- Budgeting
- Publicity and promotion
- Coordination with church programme
- Parental involvement

This chapter will deal in general with the eight steps of the planning process. Subsequent chapters will deal in more depth with a number of the areas.

Planning is a process that takes time and involves many people. The first thing to keep in mind regarding any specific weekend is that you must begin well in advance of the actual event so that there is adequate time to accomplish each step of the planning process.

Establish purpose and goals

The first step in the planning process relates to the subject of the previous chapter – purposes and goals. You shouldn't begin the planning process for a specific weekend until you've written a general purpose statement and drawn up a list of goals. If that purpose statement and the various goals are in place, then the planning for a specific trip can begin.

WHAT ARE THE REASONS FOR A YOUTH GROUP TO TRAVEL, GO ON
WEEKENDS AWAY OR HAVE COMMUNITY PROJECTS?

1. Getting acquainted in a "neutral" setting. Many of us work with young people who are non-churchgoers, and "getting away from it all" (church, family, school, the city, suburbia, etc.) provides a setting in which the group can become

better acquainted with other young people.
2. We all need a break from the rush of life wherever we are, and just being away provides an opportunity for personal renewal.
3. To avoid roles such as "son of the minister" getting in the way of building relationships.
4. Time restrictions – such as the need for youth programmes to end by 7.30 p.m. for the evening service – are not as much of a problem on a weekend away.
5. It gives a chance to deal with some important questions and issues over a concentrated period of time. Bible study and discussions have a chance to settle in the mind overnight with time for more discussion the next day.
6. Young people on trips are able to meet new friends from other churches, towns, and areas, which can be rewarding for them.
7. They and their leaders may get new ideas about their own youth group by sharing with other groups.
8. Education through experience is real on a trip. "Reconciliation", "separation", "community", "trust", etc. become real as they become a part of a group's experience.
9. The young people have a chance to work and serve others.

The planning process should begin at least six months in advance of the event. That may very well mean you have started the planning process for a future trip before you have completed a previous one. But it is important to be in early. Facilities may not be available if your planning begins too late; the leader you want may not be available at short notice; the finances you need may not be available without some prior fundraising efforts.

Recently I received a call from a member of a group in another church who had attended a trip I had led. She was looking for a conference centre for a weekend planned for a month from that day. While I gave her several possibilities, I told her that I seriously doubted she would find any vacancy that near to the time she wanted. (In fact she didn't find space and the trip had to be postponed for six weeks.)

Each year in July, I book the venue for our January trip, and usually by the end of August that centre is fully booked for the winter period.

Select a planning group

After setting general purposes and goals, your first step is to select a planning group. Include youngsters and adults in this group and don't make it so large that it can't function – five or six members is adequate. If necessary, have the group approved by the appropriate church group or committee.

The planning group should first look at the overall purpose statement and the list of goals, then select realistic goals based on their young people's needs. The planning group might begin by answering the kind of questions listed below.

PLANNING GROUP QUESTIONS

- Who will be attending the weekend?
- What are the interests of those who will attend?
- What are the relationship needs of those who will attend?
- What are the faith needs of those who will attend?
- What are the social issues of concern to those who will attend?
- What should be the focus of this time together?
- What goals are realistic?

After working through the appropriate questions, set specific goals for the trip. You may want to test these out with more youth and adults in the church before making a final decision.

Programme the content and style

Once the purpose and goals are clarified and agreed, consider the weekend programme content and style. Is the content "personal issue" orientated? Bible study orientated? "Social issue" orientated? The content will, of course, be directed toward accomplishing the goals you've chosen. The "style" is another important issue to discuss. What will it be?

- Small group activity
- Speaker
- Audio-visual input
- Individual study

- A combination of two or more of these styles

As you consider the weekend's style, remember that the best learning happens when people are taking part in the learning process.

Obtain leaders

Once the planning group members agree on the weekend's content and style, they will be ready to consider the leadership needs. Basically three teams of leaders are needed for any weekend: the Movement/Supply Team, a Caring Team, and the Programme Team. They should be directed by the Event Coordinator, a member of the Youth Leadership Team (see the diagram below).

Here are the responsibilities of these three teams.

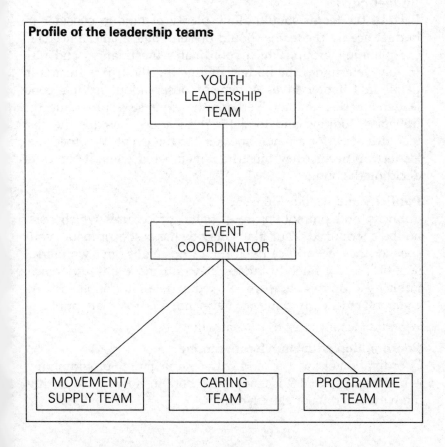

Profile of the leadership teams

YOUTH LEADERSHIP TEAM

EVENT COORDINATOR

MOVEMENT/ SUPPLY TEAM

CARING TEAM

PROGRAMME TEAM

- **Movement/Supply Team:** facilities, transport, cooking, sleeping, etc.
- **Caring Team:** individual emotional needs, discipline, etc.
- **Programme Team:** input and interaction sessions and "free time" activities. (You may want a separate "free time" team, but they should work closely with the programme team to coordinate efforts.)

On some trips the same people must manage all three areas of need; for others, you'll have different people working in the three areas. It's a good idea to have one young person and one adult on your planning team who are responsible for working with each leadership team. See Chapter Seven for ideas on recruiting leaders.

Budgeting
Each of the teams should allow plenty of time to consider its budget needs. The teams should present their financial needs to the planning group, which coordinates the finances and ultimately determines the budget. Budgeting the trip is treated in detail in Chapter Five. A general observation: having good leadership costs money. Perhaps the expense is providing the transport, lodging and food for the leaders. Perhaps the cost includes a fee for a major speaker for the event. Whatever the leadership needs, they must be remembered when it comes to deciding the budget.

Publicity and promotion
Publicity and promotion are essential procedures which must not be overlooked. Your plans may be the best ever made, your speaker the best you can get, the camp might offer wonderful facilities, but if nobody knows, it won't make any difference. Publicity and promotion are covered in detail in Chapter Six. As a general rule, early publicity never hurts a trip – late publicity can kill it.

Coordination with church programme
Coordination of the weekend with overall church programming is important so that it is compatible both in content and in timing with other major church events.

One year, our church planned a major youth weekend on the same dates as an annual parents' group trip in the church to which the young people were invited. Result: a cancelled trip. Another important factor in coordinating activities with the overall church programming is the "report back" to be given by the participants to a group within the church or to the entire congregation. Coordination is important!

Parental involvement
The final step in the planning process relates to how the parents are involved. While some parents might be in the planning group, all parents should be kept informed regarding the plans. This may take the form of a pre-trip meeting for parents (or for parents and the young people). Parental involvement might take the form of a special newsletter to the parents explaining activity policies, goals, etc. It is also important to report back to the parents as a part of the follow-up to a weekend away. The parents should know what goals were accomplished, what needs surfaced that should be discussed at home, etc. There are many possibilities and this also needs to be a part of the planning process. The planning of any weekend away is a very important process which takes time, but you'll find the reward when the trip runs smoothly and the established goals are met.

Chapter 3

Choosing the best venue

One of the first trips I planned was for a group of thirty young people. My plans called for the entire group to be together some of the time and for them to share ideas and feelings in small groups in the same room at other times. Since I hadn't seen the setting (a major mistake), I didn't realize the only room available for the programme was small and had a large, round stone fireplace in the middle. Needless to say, it was almost impossible for everyone to see the speaker. The small groups were jammed uncomfortably together. The discussions competed with noise from the other groups. I learnt about facilities the hard way!

Where to begin

The planning process becomes very practical as you start thinking about a specific weekend. You may be fortunate enough to have to decide between the countryside or the coast for a venue. On the other hand, you may have no choice at all. Whatever your situation, begin considering potential venues by getting the planning group to review the weekend's purpose and style. For instance, needing many separate rooms for small groups will determine the kind of facility you need. Or if you have a group of ten to twelve participants, you won't want a centre that seats a hundred.

Costs

Venues vary greatly in facilities and in fees they charge. Developing and maintaining a file of available activity centres gives you a variety of locations to consider.

Geographical proximity is also important in planning. (Chapter Four will deal with this in detail.) Transport costs must be considered. Also consider the amount of time necessary to get to and return from the venue. Travel time determines the amount of time left for the programme content. The proximity of the activity centre to other facilities which may be required is also important, i.e. seaside, theme park, ice rink etc.

To assemble a file on venues, get information from sources such as other local churches who may own or know of centres, denominational offices, youth organizations, e.g. Scouts, YMCA, YWCA and other community groups, town and county councils etc. See the list on page 151. Also check with national parks for available facilities. You might want to develop a file with a number of other churches in your community as a co-operative effort.

A location checklist

You can develop a checklist which will help you weigh up the relative merits of different venues for any specific trip. A check-list I've used successfully is shown on the following page.

Once you've selected a venue, use the same type of checklist for details your young people will ask you about: "How long will it take to get there?" "Can my four friends and I share a room?" "What kind of clothing and bedding do I need to take?" You probably know the kind of questions!

Activity centre expectations

Centre managers have a difficult task in maintaining policies and facilities. Knowing their expectations in advance will help in your work with them.

Tensions and frustrations grow quickly if you're not sensitive to their expectations. For instance, I once directed a trip where I thought the centre manager understood that my young people were planning to prepare the food. But it became apparent quite early that the camp manager's wife didn't share his under-standing. She quoted camp regulations regarding young people not being allowed in the kitchen as she shooed my teenage cooks away. I spent quite a bit of time sorting things out with the camp manager and his wife. Clarifying expectations saves time, effort and frustration.

The centre will have specific expectations of you and your group before, during and after the visit. It is good to clarify these expectations early in the negotiations so that you don't overlook any of them.

Venue checklist

Capacity			
Location			
Cost			
Flexibility			
Accommodation			
Facilities			
Insurance			
Safety/medical			
Other points			
Contact & address			

Camp facilities exist for the service of many different groups. As you use these facilities, you need to be considerate of the staff and the facilities. A goal my groups keep in mind is to leave the place in better condition than we found it. This is good stewardship and communicates appreciation to the staff more than anything else.

Chapter 4

Getting there: tips for transporting your group

Funny things happen when you take teenagers from a little town in Suffolk to the mountains, and funny things happen when you take twenty-five young people from the inner city to the uninhabited wilderness of Dartmoor.

Funny things happen, all right, but wonderful things happen too. Some young people find themselves. Some find new, close friends within their group – and some find God.

Lots of things happen when a Christian youth group travels away from home. Transport is one of the most important aspects of the trip that requires careful decisions.

The purpose and goals of your trip and the size of your group will affect your transport needs. Consider the interaction that takes place between young people as you travel to and from an activity centre. This interaction can be an important part of the experience, even an effective aspect of the programme. The planning group should discuss how the journey might be planned to contribute to the goals for the weekend.

Here are some strategies which might make the idea of transport as "programme" understandable:

1. If you plan to use small groups and you are travelling to the activity centre in cars, assign each group or half of each group (depending on the size of the groups) to a car. They can begin interacting with each other on their way. You may want to guide their discussions as they travel, such as encouraging them to discuss some family history, special interests, etc.
2. If you have some activities planned in pairs, assign car or bus seats so the young people are paired with their partner for the weekend.
3. If you are travelling in a large bus, make sure that activities will not distract the driver.
4. You could take an unusual mode of transport. If travelling

by train is not something your group does every day, it could be a "different" way to get to and from a weekend away. How about other modes: bicycles, horses, boats etc. Again, the weekend's purpose and goals should be well served by the way you travel together.

It is important that the planning group understands your church's travel policies. If you are not aware of any policies, ask the minister. If there is no policy, suggest that the church develop one. Some items for a policy might be:

Church travel policy

1. All travel plans should be cleared with the church leadership.
2. No person under 21 drives for a church youth group event.
3. Drivers and providers of cars must prove adequate insurance cover.
4. All drivers and vehicles must comply with all legal requirements – see the free guide *Passenger Transport provided by Voluntary Groups,* available from the Regional Traffic Commissioner's office in your area. You need to quote the reference PSV 385 when asking for it.
5. The church will be reimbursed for expenses related to the use of church transport (minibus etc).
6. Once a group has arrived at its destination there is no driving of vehicles without the consent of the leader in charge.
7. Special insurance should be obtained for the event (see also Insurance, below).
8. When travelling in several vehicles, each should be close enough to remain in sight of the next but far enough apart so as to be safe and not create a traffic problem.

Insurance

Insurance is a necessary part of the planning. Determine what cover is needed for the entire trip. Do this early in your planning process. You will probably need to extend your church's statutory public liability cover for weekends away and other youth events, and it is worth taking out a group personal accident policy. While none of us expects an accident, accidents do happen. Your young people and their families deserve adequate insurance protection.

Church minibuses and buses are becoming more and more popular forms of group transport. A church-owned vehicle can keep the cost of transport at a reasonable level. If you plan to use a church-owned vehicle, notify the person or group responsible for the vehicle several weeks before you plan to use it, so that the van or bus can be safety checked and prepared for the trip. Also be certain that your drivers have the proper licence and are experienced in driving the vehicle to be used. If the route is complicated give maps and specific directions to each driver. Make sure you have adequate space for the young people to stow their belongings and any programme materials you need for your weekend. Overcrowding and overloading a vehicle contributes to unsafe conditions, not to mention nasty attitudes. Enlist drivers well in advance of the event so that last-minute decisions regarding who will drive won't tempt you to ask anyone who happens to be available.

If you are planning to hire a coach, book well in advance. Some companies require a cash deposit. Clarify those charges before booking as well as specific times the coach is needed. Ask the company for a list of general passenger regulations. Also determine what insurance coverage they will provide for your group and decide the type of additional coverage you may need. Most commercial carriers will send a bill or present a bill in writing. Paying promptly will make you more likely to receive good service in the future.

Safety

Whether using a church bus, vans, cars or a coach, everyone should understand the need for safety. You may want to review the "Ten Commandments for Passengers" (see next page) with the planning group, adapting or changing it for your situation. Give each person in your group a copy and discuss each point before leaving.

Permission slips

Each person in your group should give you signed permission

slips. The permission slip is a simple statement which assures you that the young person's parents or guardian have given permission for the young person to attend the event. This slip should also authorize some adult on the trip to approve emergency medical treatment should that be necessary. Take the permission slips with you on the trip.

Psychologists consider travelling as a major life event – something that disrupts and alters our normal day-to-day pattern of living. Changes often come about from such experiences. The opportunity is there for your group to make lasting positive changes in your members – through the experience of a group trip.

Ten commandments for passengers

1. Thou shalt not drop litter inside or outside the bus.
2. Thou shalt not use torches or other lights in the bus.
3. Thou shalt not play radios or cassettes while on the road.
4. Thou shalt not be a backseat driver.
5. Thou shalt not stick anything (arm, leg, friend) out of the window.
6. Thou shalt sit on the seat facing forwards.
7. Thou shalt keep thy conversation at a reasonable level.
8. Thou shalt assist the driver with loading and unloading the luggage.
9. Thou shalt help to make thy trip a safe one.
10. Thou shalt express appreciation to the driver for a safe trip.

Chapter 5

Setting a budget that works

Sitting down to add up the costs of transport, food, accommodation and conference fees can be a deflating experience.

Take heart. It's really not as bad as it looks. First, you have the assurance that such trips are done all the time, in all areas, by groups of all sizes, and your members certainly should not need to be wealthy to participate in your weekend's activity.

You can add to the trip's effectiveness by cutting down on financial headaches. This chapter provides a simple budget worksheet which will help you balance costs with income.

As you consider the budget, realize once again that the weekend's purpose and goals have an impact on the financial support required. The weekend may be for a very small number (a youth officers' trip, for example) which requires some outside leadership. Or it may include a hundred teenagers using your church's own leader. Or the goal might be to include some young people who cannot afford to pay their own way. Or a goal might be to provide each young person with a copy of a book being used as the focus of study.

Obvious costs involve transport, the hire of the venue, food, etc. The tendency is to budget first for those logistical needs and then use whatever money remains for the programme costs. Yet, while it's important that logistical expenses are met, programme expenses should have priority. Otherwise you will be "short changing" the trip's goals.

Other costs
There may be costs related to pre-trip planning. It is a nice gesture to take the planning team to lunch or give them a book or something that says "thank you" for the work they do for the trip. A follow-up evaluation meeting, including refreshments, may be planned after the retreat. All such expenses should be included in the cost of the exercise.

Leadership is a cost item. Perhaps your leaders won't receive a fee, but they won't be required to pay as much or anything for the weekend. At the very least, you are partially subsidizing their participation as leaders. Include this "cost" in the pricing of the trip so that you develop a realistic budget.

Guest speakers or guest musical leaders or groups may add significantly to the weekend's cost. Don't assume you need outside speakers and groups, but be prepared to pay them at least for expenses if you do involve them. Clarify in advance the speaker's or group's financial expectations.

A budget worksheet

The sample budget worksheet on the next page will help you develop a budget that's appropriate for your trip. Get the planning group to review this sample worksheet and add or subtract categories as necessary.

The budget worksheet has two separate but equally important categories: Expenses and Income. For both of these it's necessary to estimate the number of young people you expect. Your estimate must be realistic so that you can form a realistic idea of the amount of money available for the trip. Also find out if the proposed venue has certain minimum charges which must be paid regardless of how many people attend.

HERE ARE FOUR WAYS TO KEEP COSTS DOWN:

1. Use the centre's space efficiently by filling the accommodation to capacity.
2. Find a venue where you can do your own cooking using volunteers.
3. Find a venue reasonably close to home, so that the transport costs are lower.
4. Ask participants to bring items such as paper, pencils, Bibles, etc., so that they do not need to be provided.

If the budget is tight, get the planning group to brainstorm ideas for saving money. Once you've developed a budget, the planning group must monitor it to be certain everyone stays within the budget limits.

The budget worksheet also projects a variety of income areas. It is important that the young people pay the bulk of the

Sample budget worksheet

Event _____ Date _____ No. participants _____

Estimated costs		**£**
Programme needs		_____
Leadership material needs		_____
Recreation supplies		_____
Audio-visuals		_____
Planning team expenses		_____
Venue costs:	Basic fee	_____
	Per-person fee ____ @ £____	_____
	Other	_____
Transport:	Church mini-bus	_____
	Coach hire	_____
	Petrol for cars	_____
	Other	_____
Food (if not included in venue charges)		_____
Insurance (if not included in venue charges)		_____
Other:	_____	_____
	_____	_____

TOTAL ESTIMATED EXPENSES [_____]

Expected income

Participants' fees ____ @ £____		_____
Contribution from church		_____
Fundraising event(s)		_____
Other sources:	_____	_____
	_____	_____

TOTAL ESTIMATED INCOME [_____]

BALANCE [_____]

expenses. Paying their own way helps young people to "buy in" emotionally to the experience. If they've "invested" money in the experience they will want to get their money's worth out of the event.

Keep an accurate record of everyone's registration. On the next page is a sample registration form that could be used for the larger events.

This form can be used for a variety of needs throughout the weekend. Requiring full payment before the trip is a good policy. This will keep you from playing "bill collector" after the event. It may also avoid embarrassing situations for young people who later discover they can't afford the event.

As we conclude this chapter on budgeting, it is appropriate to look ahead to the chapter on publicity and promotion. Proper budgeting depends on reaching the projected registration number. Getting people to attend the activity depends on good advance publicity.

Event registration sheet

Name	Fee[1]	Paid[2]	Present[3]	Group[4]	Room[5]	Forms[6]	Other[7]

How to fill in the columns

1. Fee   Enter here the amount to be paid. This may vary if you offer a discount for early book-
            ing or if more than one member of a family attend.
2. Paid   Tick this column when full payment has been received.
3. Present Tick here when the person has arrived ready for departure.
4. Group   If people are assigned to small groups, number the groups and note the appropriate
            group number here.
5. Room   Record here the room number allocated to each participant.
6. Forms   Tick this column when you have received the signed permission slip from each partici-
            pant.
7. Other   An extra space to use for any other information you may wish to record.

Chapter 6

Publicity and promotion: how to increase attendance at your weekend away

On arriving home from school, Linda browses through the day's post. She flips quickly through the bills and a handful of plain-looking letters addressed to her parents. Her eyes open wide when she gets to the piece of post that looks like a burger, complete with arty sesame seeds and a small bug sitting near her name and address.

"My youth group's at it again," she says, chuckling to herself. She dumps her books and the rest of the post on a corner of the kitchen table and takes a closer look at the paper burger.

As she opens this piece of youth group "junk mail", the first thing she reads is a large headline. "Attack a Big Mac." She reads on. The notice introduces a forthcoming youth group starve-a-thon weekend to raise money for a world famine relief organization.

That weekend at church, well placed posters, attractive reminders of the event, caught her attention. Not only did the posters give information, but they helped everyone in the group get excited about the forthcoming starve-a-thon.

In the weeks to come, Linda would receive two more creative mailings, be telephoned by a friend telling her about the event, read about it in the church bulletin and hear announcements in church and her youth group meetings. Her parents would even receive an informative letter and an invitation to a special "parents-of-potential-starve-a-thon-people" meeting.

Linda was impressed. In the past, she had never really known much about forthcoming events. This time, though, she felt as if she were a part of the trip already. And she couldn't wait to take part.

Publicity pays

A planning team's work will be wasted if it isn't communicated adequately to the group. The best planned trips will never succeed if the advance publicity and promotion isn't complete, attractive and persuasive. Besides just listing the date, time, place, cost etc., a good publicity poster or mailing should communicate the trip's theme and general objective. Good promotion motivates.

Timing is an extremely important factor in the planning of any promotional effort. The planning group should arrive at its decisions early enough so that the first announcement of the trip appears at least two and a half months before the event. The planning group can list in a church newsletter or on a bulletin board in the church hall the calendar of the events for the year even before detailed, specific planning has taken place. As soon as you know the date for your trip, work backwards – developing your own promotion timetable, which might look something like the example below.

The planning group should also determine the target group for the specific event. What age range is the trip designed to

---

Sample promotion timetable

10 weeks before. Initial announcement: verbal and brief written notice in church newsletter, posters, etc.

8 weeks before. Detailed notice distributed to potential participants (see publicity checklist on page 26 for points to be included).

6 weeks before. Telephone contacts (organize a phone-a-thon to potential participants).

1 month before. Deadline for "early booking" deal which may include a special price or incentive.

3 weeks before. Another notice – give more details as available (see publicity checklist for points to be included).

2 weeks before. Personal contact follow-up.

1 week before. Booking deadline.

serve? Who within that age range is it designed to serve? Also consider such questions as:

How can we assemble all the names of potential participants, especially if it is open to more than just our church youth group?

Is there a capacity which restricts how many can attend, and on what basis is the selection made? First come, first served? Priority to church members? Priority to a certain age?

Publicity checklist
Whether you design a promotional mailing leaflet, an article for the church newsletter, a poster or press release for your local newspaper, the checklist on the next page will help you include the necessary information.

There is almost never a danger of providing too much publicity. Too often the lack, lateness or incompleteness of communication causes these trips to be poorly attended. Even though a member of your planning group should coordinate publicity and promotion, each member of the planning group should take an active part in the promotion effort.

More ideas

Posters placed in the church and community where young people will see them can increase interest and participation. Perhaps you will want to launch a poster contest early in the promotion schedule and award a free trip to the winning design. Perhaps you can offer a discount to each person who enters the poster contest. Maybe a business person in your church would donate a prize for the contest winner.

Another promotion technique is to give a special discount or prize to each member of your group who signs up five other participants. You could even give a discount to each of a group of five who book together. Take note of special promotional techniques used in successful businesses. Don't be afraid to use those ideas in your own promotions.

Word of mouth is best
Publicity and promotion are extremely important in any event's success formula. Even though mailings and posters are crucial,

Publicity checklist

Use this checklist when preparing posters and mailings two months before the event. Use it again for publicity three weeks before the event.

Theme _____

Purpose _____

Goals _____

Who is it intended for? _____

Venue _____

Cost_____

Booking deadline _____

Booking procedure _____

Cancellation policy _____

Permission slip for booking _____

Organizer's name, address, phone no. _____

_____

Additional list three weeks before the event

Who has already booked? _____

Phone number of venue _____

Name of speaker/music group/film etc. _____

What to bring: sleeping bag, swimwear, torch etc. _____

_____

the best promotion is still one-to-one personal communication. The best "recruiters" are your young people themselves as they become excited about the trip and spread the news to their friends. The planning group begins this communication process as they themselves get excited about the event. Mailings and posters provide potential participants with the information they need to consider their own involvement in the weekend's activity. But the dimension of personal one-to-one communication is the key to promotional success. Printed publicity usually can't carry the entire promotional load.

OTHER WAYS TO ENCOURAGE ONE-TO-ONE COMMUNICATION

- Give each person who books a badge or sticker to wear which says something like YES, or I'M GOING, etc.
- Make a display, on a bulletin board where the young people will see it, listing the number of people who are attending and/or their names.

The aim of promotion and publicity is to build interest in and anticipation of the event. Remember, effective promotion and publicity take time and careful planning. Effort is the key.

A weekend journal

Your members may well experience some of the best times of their lives on your weekend. These times will be too good to forget, so get a volunteer or two from the group to write a trip journal.

At the end of each day, the journal writer should sit down and write out everything that happened that day. Include good and bad things, laughs and miseries, fun and boring times. Be sure to include lots of the young people's names. Write the journal like a diary – a separate entry for each day. Don't let anyone else see your journal entries.

When you return from the trip, type out the journal and have it photocopied. You may want to add some artwork on the cover. Then, set aside time in one of your regular meetings to pass out the journals.

Your journal could become one of your prized possessions, read year after year.

A slide or video show

Your trip can be shared, preserved and recycled through the use of video or slides. A simple video or slide programme can be extremely effective to communicate your group's activities to others. It's also great to show the programme a year later to your own group to generate enthusiasm for your next trip.

All you'll need are videotape or slides from your weekend and a couple of tape recorders. Put together, these will let your audience experience sights and actual comments from your members.

Always be sure one of your members takes plenty of slides. Include all phases of group life in the photography. Don't ignore ordinary things like meals and people sitting around. Sometimes those simple times are the most memorable.

After you return from your trip, set up a time when all the members can talk individually with an interviewer. The interviewer can be either the leader or a member, but should have some skill at interviewing. The interview time can be during your regular group meeting time, or you may wish to plan a special get-together for it.

Your interviewer should have a number of questions prepared to ask each member. The questions should be geared to the slides or video images you have from the trip. Some sample questions might be: "How did you like the closing worship service?", "What did you think of the small group experiences?", "What was it like eating food your friends cooked?" and "How did you like the hike we took on Friday night?"

Also ask some general questions about the value of the trip or camp. Examples: "What did you get out of it?" and "How did you see God working in our group and during the weekend?" Your interviewer should also feel free to ad lib some questions. Avoid questions that could be answered with a "yes" or "no".

Take each member separately to a quiet spot for the interview session. Use a good tape recorder and microphone. Try not to spend more than four or five minutes with each member. This will make editing easier.

At the end, play the tape, and make note of good quotes from members. This job will be easier if you use a recorder with a footage counter: you just need to mark down the footage numbers of the good quotes and they're simple to find later. Be sure to include at least one quote from each member; don't leave anyone out.

After you've selected the best comments, arrange on paper the quotes and the scenes. You needn't follow chronological order. For longer comments, you may plan to use four or five scenes. Sometimes you may wish to stay on the same one for two or three comments. But, as a general rule, plan to have each scene on the screen for only a few seconds.

When you've placed your selected comments in their best order, you may want to write some additional narrative. Keep this to a minimum and use it to tie thoughts together. Your audience is much more interested in the voices and comments of all your members.

Next, record you narrator's introduction. Or you may want to begin with one of the actual comments from a member. Then proceed to put all the comments and other narration in the proper order on your master tape.

FOR A TAPE – SLIDE SHOW

You'll need two tape recorders or a machine with twin cassette decks. Cue up the selected quote on one machine. Set up the other machine to record and start both machines. Some machines can be linked by a cable connection that allows direct recording, thus avoiding picking up unwanted background sounds with a microphone. Continue to master-record every comment and bit of narration in the right order. You may want to end the programme with a little music. Then hand the master tape and slides over to whoever is to be the presenter, who will spend the necessary time familiarizing himself with the proper spots on the tape to change the slides on the screen. This must be well rehearsed.

Use a good tape player for your actual presentation. If it is not powerful enough, you may need to run it through an auxiliary amplifier to get the necessary volume.

This project takes some work, but is tremendously effective

with audiences. It also provides a permanent record of your group's experiences together.

Using the media

Have you ever considered using your local newspaper or radio station to publicize your houseparty or weekend away? It will certainly help motivate your regular members to see or hear the group mentioned, and it may help jolt some of your more irregular members into action, especially if you have a large group. It will probably also generate interest for potential new members of the group. Knowing and heeding a few simple ground rules will enable your group to prepare publicity material that will be attractive to the media.

Your goal should be to produce publicity material that the media will use without excessive editing. The less rewriting the media have to do, the better. But don't be upset if the news release that you laboured over for hours doesn't appear exactly as you prepared it. Many in the media rewrite everything that crosses their desks.

When preparing a news release, remember always to include the *who, what, where, when, why* and *how* at the beginning. Never wait until the end of your release to "spring the surprise" of important information. News should be delivered in the fashion of an "inverted triangle", to use journalists' jargon. That is, the most important information appears at the beginning and least important details are found at the end. This allows the editor to use as much of the story as he has room for – knowing that wherever he's chosen to cut your story, he's hacked the less important material.

Use short paragraphs. Two or three sentences are usually plenty, for example:

The Cranfield Young People's Fellowship is taking to the hills next month. This will be their first trip to the Brecon Beacons and they have a full programme planned. Canoeing, mountaineering and a trip down a disused coalmine feature high on the itinerary.

The theme for the week is trust. Tim Harris, leader of the group, says, "We expect to find ourselves needing to exercise a lot of trust in the activities and hope to learn something about trusting God too."

The group expect to number around 25 young people from Cranfield and Harbourne who will depart on 5 May, returning 9 May. For further enquiries about CYPF phone Cranfield 2741.

Always type your releases. Editors hate handwriting – even when it's legible. Double-space your material, and type only on one side of the paper.

Begin typing halfway down your first sheet. This allows space above for the editor to write a headline. Always number consecutive pages.

Never deliver a carbon copy or a photocopy to the newspaper. It's an insult to any editor to believe that the other newspaper got the original copy. When an original typed release reaches the editor, he's impressed that you prepared the material especially for him. A photocopy signals to the editor that all the other media in town have the same release, and he may not be interested in your mass-produced "news".

If you plan to use more than one newspaper or radio/TV station, type a different release for each of them. It's a lot of work, but you'll have a much better chance of having your releases used.

Your stories for large local daily newspapers should usually be shorter and more concise than the stories you'd write for the smaller newspapers.

For most events, the best time to submit your releases is one week beforehand. Smaller auxiliary stories could precede and follow the main story, if the local media are likely to use such material.

Studies have shown that readers give much more attention to photographs than to printed words. So, whenever you can, submit photos with your stories. Use black and white prints, not slides, colour snapshots or negatives.

Always include caption information with the photo. It's best to attach a slip of paper to the back of the photo carrying typed information about who or what appears in the picture.

Always put your name and phone number on your releases in case an editor has a question. Give the newspaper or radio station a call if you have any questions about submitting a news release. They'd be happy to help you.

Chapter 7

Leaders and helpers

Volunteer helpers – those adults without whom youth events would fizzle out – are a vital part of the weekend away process. They give their time and energy to make things happen in a church youth group.

Carefully consider and plan their role in the experience. In my early years of planning and directing trips I suffered several uncomfortable experiences with volunteer helpers. I encountered volunteers who wanted to run the exercise like an army camp. Others who weren't youth-orientated saw the experience as a burden rather than an opportunity to learn and grow with the group. Yet many volunteers through the years have found new friendships with young people which have led to long-term supportive relationships.

Perhaps the greatest danger in the use of volunteer helpers is taking them for granted. We tend to "use" them without giving them the same careful attention we give the participants. This chapter will help you make the adult volunteers an integral part of the event. The trip can be a growth-producing event for them too.

Finding good volunteers

Who should the adult volunteers be? Perhaps you have regular helpers who work with the youth group who will be involved in the trip you are planning. Or maybe you are the volunteers and you're reading this book to hone your own planning skills. People who become volunteers should meet several basic requirements. Volunteer helpers should:

- respect young people;
- be willing to grow in their understanding of them;
- be growing in their own faith experience.

If you are responsible for getting helpers, begin the process in the planning team by listing the qualities the team feels are important for youth leaders, for instance: open, fun to be with, has good Bible knowledge, outdoor type, knows the group.

Then brainstorm a list of potential people from your church. Don't eliminate any names yet. You may find new people, never previously considered; you may also find someone you thought didn't like youth weekends will say "yes". It is essential that the planning team are committed to the choice of people invited to be helpers.

After you have listed potential helpers based upon the list of qualities, begin to list the duties helpers will have to carry out on this specific event. Your list is likely to include some of the following:

- Drive car/minibus
- Supervise catering
- Supervise sleeping areas
- Lead Bible study
- Lead recreation
- Organize hike

This list will help you meet the specific needs of the weekend with specific abilities. After listing the expectations, prepare a "Leadership Need Statement" (see below) which includes the specific needs which you will be asking a person to fulfil. This "job description" will be helpful as you approach particular individuals.

Leadership need statement
To make our youth weekend on November 3–5 a success, we need an adult leader who will:

1. *Provide transport*
2. *Supervise the kitchen*
3. *Supervise the sleeping areas*

We would appreciate your consideration of this invitation to serve. If you accept, you will be invited to an orientation and training session in October so that you can understand more fully the trip and your responsibilities.
   WE NEED YOU!

Note: A different Leadership Need Statement would be prepared for each separate job description. The recruitment would be done face to face and this statement would be given to the potential helper at that time.

Who makes a good volunteer?

Parents may be good helpers. Parents may be terrible helpers. People over 65 years of age may be good helpers. People over 65 years of age may be terrible helpers. People between 28 and 35 may be good helpers. People between 28 and 35 may be terrible helpers. Get the picture?

"Who" the helpers "are" is important as it relates to the initial qualities listed in your brainstorming session. Don't eliminate any potential volunteers because they are "parents" or are "too old". Don't automatically assume "young adults" will be the best ones. Think deeply about potential helpers!

BEFORE THE EVENT

☐ Recruit helpers face to face.

☐ Provide them with written leadership need/job descriptions.

☐ Orientate them to the trip. Gather all the adult leadership, at which time the planning team should share their planning process, the goals, the role of the leaders, the "rules" of the weekend, etc.

☐ Train them. If they are to have "programme" responsibilities, lead them through all or part of the curriculum which they will be expected to coordinate.

☐ Review "behaviour expectations" for participants and how leaders are to communicate those expectations.

☐ Review needs for which they are responsible.

☐ Worship together through Bible study and prayer.

DURING THE EVENT

☐ Plan a regular leadership time to review the event's progress.

☐ Support the leaders informally.

☐ Encourage leaders to be mutually supportive.

☐ Provide room and board at no cost to the volunteer helpers. Transport too, if possible.
☐ Publicly thank them at the conclusion of the event, before the group goes home.
☐ Seek their evaluation of the exercise.

AFTER THE EVENT

☐ Thank them with a written note.
☐ Thank them publicly – by listing names in the church newsletter, maybe, or recognizing them in a worship service.
☐ Have a follow-up evaluation session, perhaps with the planning team.
☐ Ask for written recommendations to be used as input for future retreats.

Chapter 8

Rules

Have you ever been to a youth event where you felt the group's primary goal was to break the rules? The adult-written rules were a challenge to the young people, saying to them, "We dare you to break these." Rules should never be the focal point of a youth group or youth event. Good rules remain in the background to provide structure and reasonable limits so that members of the group can live positively together in a Christian atmosphere. Here are some guidelines for setting effective rules for youth fellowships and events.

Be positive

Start with a positive attitude by setting an atmosphere which expects the best of both young people and adults. Too often we expect the worst and try to legislate against it. A large number of negatively stated rules says to the young people, "We expect the worst from you. We don't believe you can be responsible, so we're listing these restrictions because we expect a terrible outcome." Sure enough, they will meet their leaders' expectations.

Even the act of discipline can be a positive experience when it's used to teach instead of punish or put down. What happens when a rule is broken? If the young rule-breaker is singled out, embarrassed and put down, both the group and the individual suffer tremendous damage. In the biblical context, to discipline means to correct or teach. It does not mean to punish, put down or destroy a young person's self-esteem. When a rule is broken, sit down with the rule-breaker, person to person, outside the group and discuss both the problem and the appropriate consequences.

Another aspect of being positive in rule setting is to ask, "What is the loving thing to do?" Recall Paul's saying that love is the fulfilment of the law. The end result of every rule should be, "What is loving?" Granted, love should not be sentimental or wavering. Following through on prescribed consequences to breaking a rule is love.

Be precise

Say what you mean; be brief, be precise. When rules are set by both young people and adults, be clear about what is expected. Keep your list of rules brief. State the consequences if the rules are broken.

Get adults and the youth group to set rules at a meeting. Go over the rules and consequences for special events as well as weekly fellowships. If parents feel certain rules need to be added or modified, let those recommendations be considered and appropriately implemented.

Be prepared

Rule preparation has several stages. First, be sure that the rules are set by responsible young people and adult leaders. Next, help the entire group make the rules their own by allowing everyone to say "yes" to them.

Prepare both parents and young people before a weekend away by publishing the rules in the information about the event. Before our youth group leaves on a trip, parents and participants gather with the leaders immediately prior to leaving. The leaders explain the trip's details and rules. Everyone, including the parents, helpers and young people, hears the rules and the consequences of breaking them. Everyone is prepared, so that no one can say, "I did not know." The rules are also printed in the programme booklet for the trip so that everyone knows what to expect.

The most major consequence we have used (beyond a helper personally confronting someone about breaking a rule and working it through with him or her) is sending a rule-breaker home. We explain to the parents that they will be responsible for providing their young person's transport home. In over twelve years, I have had to resort to that measure only twice. Both times were learning and growing experiences for the young people concerned.

More pointers for setting rules

Have enough adult supervision. Our practice is that for every ten young people of one sex, we have one adult of the same sex. This rule is particularly important when planning trips, conventions or outings with other church groups. When other groups are involved, the young people need to understand that they come under the supervision of adults from their own congregation. It is very difficult to expect adults to supervise young people from other churches if no adults from those churches are present.

Hand over supervision to responsible young people. There comes a point where the most effective group discipline is handing it over to the young people themselves. The objective is to get to a stage where they maintain discipline and the adults give support.

A controlled environment limits temptation. If there are large portions of unscheduled, unsupervised, unplanned time during an event, you can count on problems arising. When we plan an event, every minute of it is accounted for. That doesn't mean we plan activities for every bit of the time, but it does mean that we know what is going on at every moment. When we go on a trip, we don't turn unsupervised youngsters loose on the town. There are planned and scheduled activities at each point in the programme. At night, it is clear where the girls sleep and where the boys sleep, and those sleeping areas are out of bounds to people of the opposite sex.

Decide whose problem it is. On one youth weekend, one of the parent helpers saw his son and a girl holding hands. The parent lost his temper with his son in front of the entire group. It was devastating for the parent–child relationship as well as for the group itself. Much of the problem in this particular incident was with the parent. Adults need to ask themselves two questions when they see misbehaviour: "Is this something I personally disapprove of, but which is within the limits of the rules?" and "Is this behaviour a clear violation of group rules?" Times when adults come down too hard on the young people can be avoided initially by determining immediately whose problem it is.

Always get the facts directly from those involved. On one of our trips, I found out that some of the boys had cigarettes with them. No one had smoked any of them, but their presence was well known to many of the youngsters. Instead of asking, "Is this true?" or "Can you tell me more?" I asked them to give me the facts of the situation. I also explained that the trip could not go on until the situation was resolved.

In one-to-one conversation, I got the facts of the situation. The cigarettes were disposed of, appropriate disciplinary action was taken and the trip went on without incident. Getting the facts directly from the people involved was indispensable in being able to work out fair discipline.

Love rules all
The ultimate question to ask yourself in setting solid rules is "What is the loving thing to do?" as Paul emphasizes in his letters. Rules point towards *agape*, the love that builds people's worth and self-esteem. It finds worth there even when the people themselves do not feel worthy. *Agape* is tough love that seeks to discipline, teach and correct within the biblical norms. There are times when the letter of the law gives way to the spirit which is love.

Rules are important. People are more important. Act out of the depth of love – a tough love – as you work on rules with your youth group.

Chapter 9

When you have a problem with someone

I found myself out in the freezing night before I knew where I was and what was happening. I hadn't even stopped to tie my shoelaces. "Tom's missing" were the two words that started me on my middle-of-the-night trek.

This was Tom's first winter trip with our group. From the start, I wasn't sure I liked his cocky, macho attitude.

I crunched across the frozen ground towards the lights in the recreation building. After what seemed like an eternity, I reached the icicle-covered building. As I walked through the door I recognized one of the voices as that of the guest speaker. He and his wife were trouncing Tom and his girlfriend in a game of cards. They were talking about one of the weekend's topics: dating relationships.

With still sweaty palms, I crunched back through the frozen snow to my now-cold sleeping bag. There had been no confrontation. No punishment. No action. I'd been reprieved – this time.

In the years since that experience, I've faced quite a few sticky problems. And I've seen other youth leaders react in a thousand different ways when they were confronted with a tense situation. Those reactions range from seeing a leader fling one of his rebellious kids against a wall to hearing a leader, in his one-of-the-gang voice, tell some of his group members to keep quiet about the beer drinking and promise not to do it again.

Such problems are universal. No one is immune. Just when you think things are going smoothly you are proved wrong. Someone is drinking beer. Or you stumble across passionate lovers. Or three of your macho types "light up" in front of other group members. There's no end to the creative hassle that may crop up when you're in charge.

An attitude check

Your attitude to problem situations and the young people who get tangled up in them can often determine whether the end result is guilt, notoriety or spiritual growth.

Ask yourself these questions: What should the relationship be between a leader and young people who cause problems? How responsible do you feel for the behaviour of your young people? Do you feel that you can handle most problem situations yourself? Or do you feel comfortable letting other people help you deal with your problem people? What's your minister's attitude to young people who cause problems? Your church's attitude? The parents' attitude?

"The mark of a spiritually mature youth leader is his or her ability to focus on the youth and not on himself when problems come," says one experienced teacher of youth ministry principles. "Too many youth leaders put their feelings and their responsibility as leaders before the people with the problem. Many leaders are ruthless in dealing with a problem because they want everything to return to normal as quickly as possible. But they should be more concerned about talking with the young person and listening to why he did what he did. We need to look at those problems as a sign of pain, that something's not right."

While you can't handle any two problems or any two young people in exactly the same way, there are several principles that will apply to almost any situation you'll face. Here are a few:

- The world's future doesn't depend on how powerfully and decisively you react in a problem situation. Stay calm, take a few deep breaths. Sometimes it's even helpful to put everything on "hold" for a couple of minutes while you think things through. If so, tell the problem person you need a little time – then let him or her do some thinking and evaluating too. Realize that your relationship with the problem person after the incident is more important to his or her future behaviour and spiritual growth than the problem itself.

- If you're relatively new to youth work, you've probably noticed that "older" leaders seem to handle problems better than you. Of course, experience is a valuable asset. But, more important, the people in the group have learnt to trust and respect him or her. Caring enough to look beneath the surface of a problem to where a young person is hurting is a big chunk of the problem-solving process.

- It's better to deal with a problem while it's still fresh than to wait till later. Dealing with a problem as soon as you've gathered your thoughts can prevent a guilt reaction from building up in the problem person. In some cases, a prompt reaction can put the brakes on a publicity flood, where the problem people gain notoriety from others who hear about whatever happened.
- Don't make threats or give ultimatums unless you can follow them through. One leader threatened to send two boys and three girls home if they went swimming instead of attending one of the seminars. They went swimming. And when the leader tried to make good his threat, he found his vicar unwilling to remove them. Everyone lost something from that experience: the young people, the leader, even the vicar.
- Reduce the risk of potential problems through careful planning. One group that spends several weeks on the road each summer in a music group doesn't allow the girls to wear running shorts or skimpy T-shirts. The boys aren't allowed to wear running shorts either. And shirts are required. "Those rules have almost eliminated the sexually-related hassles we used to have," the leader comments. "And the group don't seem to mind the rules. In fact, I think most of them are relieved."
- Include other youth leaders in your problem-solving process. Talking about specific problems with other leaders can help you be more objective and keep your emotions and ego from getting too heavily involved. The added perspective can be a valuable asset in working with the young person to nurture their personal and spiritual growth.

When you have to act

Even though each problem and each young person is different, there is a valuable person-orientated process you can follow. This four-step problem-solving process includes the person or persons involved in the problem, the leader, and potentially the people affected by the problem. It is designed to get at the causes of the problem, its effects and consequences by using listening, feedback and clarifying skills. At each step in the process, the young person is at the centre of attention.

A FOUR-STEP PROBLEM-SOLVING PROCESS

1. It's important to identify and clarify all aspects of the problem, its effects on the group, on individuals, on property and how it relates to the people who created it. For instance, it's important to know whether the problem arose because the group were releasing anxiety, striving for attention, for notoriety, and so on.
2. Identify what led to the problem. How did it come about? Did the events that led to the problem occur spontaneously? Or was the problem the result of prior planning and premeditation? Who else might have had a part in creating the situation that led to the problem?
3. Once you've identified the problem and what caused it, look at its consequences. Who is affected by it? The whole group? The entire church? Property? Ask questions, so that you know people understand exactly the problem and its consequences. If you make assumptions about what the group understand and feel, you may infer things that they don't intend to convey.
4. It's important to find out in their words what they see as potential solutions to the problem and its consequences. What would they do to correct the problem?

Who else should you tell?

As far as relating the problem to the rest of the youth group, you need to make a value judgement after talking with the person or persons involved in the problem. What will airing the problem do to relationships within the group and within the church community?

Whether or not you should include parents in the process

depends on the nature of the problem. The most effective guide-line is to involve the parents if the young person feels they can be constructive to the outcome. On the other hand, a parent may be quick to administer punishment that's far out of propor-tion to what happened.

However, if you see the problem as continuing or serious, like smoking, drinking or vandalism, you may have to bring the parents in as a resource in order to get something constructive done. If so, tell the young person, "I'm asking your parents to become involved because I feel you need their help to deal with this problem effectively."

Regardless of who you include in the process, it's your responsibility to inform the church leadership about the prob-lem before they hear of it from secondary (and usually unreliable) sources. Explain what happened and how you han-dled the situation.

Practise, practise, practise

Your problem-solving effectiveness will get pretty watered down if you wait till you have a crisis before working through this process with your young people. A practical way of prepar-ing for potential problems is through using role plays. For example, choose a potential problem situation (slipping out at night, drinking, disregarding group rules). Work through the "problem" with the entire group using the process outlined earlier.

Before you role play potential problems with your group, meet with other leaders and work on listening skills, feedback methods, question-asking skills and clarifying techniques. All are vital to getting at the root of what the young person feels, thinks and values.

Your careful consideration and planning for problem situa-tions will pay off in the lives of your members. Seasoned youth workers have found that the greatest growth often arises not from smooth times but from those painful problem episodes.

Chapter 10

Follow-up

The value of any weekend away is not limited to the new experiences and friendships gained during the actual event. The real "pay-off" comes in the days, weeks, months and years following the event as young people live out what they have learnt and turn new friendships into long-term understandings and commitments. It is for this reason that any planning group should consider a deliberate follow-up process to the experience as a definite part of its responsibilities.

Evaluation

Evaluation is the term we often use when attempting to measure a trip's success. Some evaluation should take place before you leave the venue as well as further evaluation some time after the experience.

Evaluation immediately after the trip gives you general reactions and feelings regarding the input and interaction. The immediate evaluation may target some persons who had a particularly traumatic experience, either positive or negative. The caring team should pay special attention to these people following the event. The value of the later evaluation is to determine the ongoing impact of the experience. Both evaluations should be aimed at determining if the purpose and goals established by the planning group have been met or to what degree they were met.

Evaluation also gives the planning team information which will help them plan the next weekend away. Each planning team should have the evaluative input from previous experiences. Don't just do things the same way because they've always been successful. Be willing as a planning group to study and understand the evaluations from past trips. Also be willing to venture out into new areas which might produce better results.

Evaluation Exercise

Use a scale of 1 – 10 (10 = "best") to respond to questions 1 and 2.

1. How would you rate your overall experience at this event? ☐
2. How do you react to specific sessions?

Friday night
Icebreaker ☐
Session 1 ☐
Friday surprise ☐

Saturday
Breakfast ☐
Exercise session ☐
Icebreaker ☐
Session 2 ☐
Lunch ☐
Afternoon activity ☐
Session 3 ☐
Dinner ☐
Guest speaker, group ☐
Session 4 ☐
Late film ☐

Sunday
Early quiet time ☐
Breakfast ☐
Exercise session ☐
Worship ☐

3. What personal reactions or feelings do you have about this event?

_____

4. What did you like best about the event?

_____

5. What would you change?

_____

6. What suggestions do you have?

_____

Sign your name here if you wish _____

Opposite is a sample of one church's event evaluation form, which the young people complete just before the closing worship service on the Sunday morning.

Coming down from the mountain

"Mountaintop" experiences on a weekend away are fantastic. However, it is important to work on "coming down" as one leaves the event and heads for home. It seems that when we get into a peak experience on a weekend away it is sometimes tough to re-enter the home situation. This state can sometimes bring on a reaction which can be quite depressing. But it doesn't have to happen. You and your group can take the experiences at the special event and blend them into your home situation. Here are some steps to facilitate this process.

First, each person should gather with other members of the group and spend some time "debriefing". Begin by focusing on a personal reflection of the warmest moment of the event. Ponder this question, for example: "What was the best thing about this event?" It might help to write down that memory. After everyone has recorded or focused on that one aspect of the event, each person shares it with the group. If the memory is too personal, go on to the next person.

The next step towards re-entry will be the group's brainstorming on how your group can use some of those experiences in your youth programme. This may be a small idea or memorable moment. You might remember something that another young person shared in a small brainstorming session. You might begin this step as individual reflection and then move into a group sharing and discussion. During the session, be sure to write every idea on a flip chart or blackboard. You will be amazed how the space will be filled with ideas. As one person remembers a useful idea, it will trigger a new idea in someone else.

The last step draws these highlights into your programme. Get the group members to develop the ideas for use in meetings over the following weeks.

Mountaintop experiences need not be left on the mountain. This procedure I've described can make them starting points in youth ministry long after coming back to earth.

Chapter 11

Planning checklists

The checklists on pages 48 – 50 are guides to help you develop an approach that's appropriate for your particular event. They should be used by the event coordinator – the person selecting and working with the planning group. The checklist on pages 48 – 49 is arranged according to the planning needs as described in this book. Each task or need on the checklist will direct the planning group or the coordinator to more tasks which must be completed. As the planning group meets, you may want to reproduce the updated checklist so that the entire group can see the current situation and feel good when something is completed.

The checklist may also become a time planner. After each general category or specific task, you may wish to write in the appropriate date to have the task completed or under way. Various chapters in this book give guidance as to the timing of planning stages. The checklists may help you to keep track of progress.

Planning checklist

Purpose and goals
☐ Select planning group
☐ Establish purpose and goals
☐ Appoint and orientate movement/supply team
☐ Appoint and orientate caring team
☐ Appoint and orientate programme team

Venue
☐ Review available sites
☐ Select site
☐ Determine budget needs
☐ Visit site, if possible with programme team

cont'd

Transport
- ☐ Determine available methods
- ☐ Review church transport policy
- ☐ Select appropriate method
- ☐ Orientate leadership
- ☐ Determine budget needs
- ☐ Check insurance
- ☐ Organize safety check if using church vehicle(s)

Budget
- ☐ Estimate expenses using worksheet on page 20
- ☐ Determine income sources with planning group
- ☐ Determine fee for participants
- ☐ Estimate income
- ☐ Determine the working budget
- ☐ Be responsible for incoming and outgoing funds
- ☐ Provide written summary to planning group after event

Publicity and promotion
- ☐ Determine target group
- ☐ Prepare appropriate timetable
- ☐ Design or obtain promotional materials
- ☐ Distribute promotional materials

Rules
- ☐ Review church policies
- ☐ Review venue policies
- ☐ Establish your guidelines with planning group
- ☐ Communicate guidelines to participants

Programme design
- ☐ Research and develop needs to which event should respond
- ☐ Select someone to design the event
- ☐ Alternatively, select an outline from this book or another source
- ☐ List personnel and materials needed
- ☐ Make sure plans have the church's approval
- ☐ Decide and publicize event timetable

Follow-up
- ☐ Prepare caring team to follow up as necessary
- ☐ Decide on any post-event sessions
- ☐ Prepare written evaluation for future reference

Planning checklist for the movement/supply team

☐ Review purpose and goals
☐ Review the team responsibilities
☐ Consider possible sites
☐ Visit those to be considered
☐ Study facilities and costs
☐ Recommend site to planning group
☐ Determine transport needs
☐ Check insurance needs
☐ Study catering needs
☐ Submit budget recommendation to planning group

Planning checklist for the caring team

☐ Review purpose and goals
☐ Consider personal and group needs
☐ Develop plans for response to needs
☐ Prepare for follow-up needs

Planning checklist for the programme team

☐ Review purpose and goals
☐ Review suggested programme content as determined by planning group
☐ Discuss leadership needs
☐ Contribute to programme development
☐ Recommend budget to planning group
☐ Plan evaluation of programme

Chapter 12

Two sample event programmes

The first programme (page 52) is a typical format for a weekend trip which allows for a balance between input sessions and optional times. The second (page 53) is quite different. If you use it, be certain that your adult leaders and helpers have a restful week before the event. You may want to plan the trip for a three-day weekend when the following Monday is a bank holiday.

Both can work well. The first one always has to contend with the young people's reluctance to "settle down" the first night. The second does not have that problem.

These sample programmes are presented as a starting point. As your planning group considers the purpose, goals, programme style, content, leadership, etc. they must also consider the overall plan. Introduce it to your young people in advance of the weekend, especially if it is out of the ordinary for your group. A key phrase to remember once you've developed a plan is "Be flexible"!

A typical event programme

Friday

6.00 p.m.	Departure from church
7.30 p.m.	Stop for a snack
8.15 p.m.	Continue journey
9.00 p.m.	Arrive at venue and move in
10.00 p.m.	Session 1 (getting acquainted with one another, brief introduction to the theme)
11.00 p.m.	Time to chat, unpack and settle down
Midnight	Lights out

Saturday

8.00 a.m.	Breakfast
9.00 a.m.	Session 2 (theme presentation and development, interaction, maybe music)
10.30 a.m.	Time for optional activities or rest
Midday	Lunch
1.00 p.m.	Session 3 (continued theme development)
2.00 p.m.	Time for optional activities or doing your own thing
5.30 p.m.	Tea
6.30 p.m.	Session 4 (continued theme development)
7.30 p.m.	Celebration time (games, sketches, maybe a talent show)
9.00 p.m.	Special event (video, music group, etc.)
10.30 p.m.	Refreshments and free time
Midnight	Lights out

Sunday

9.00 a.m.	Breakfast
10.00 a.m.	Session 5 (theme conclusion, worship)
11.00 a.m.	Tidy up, pack up
Midday	Lunch
1.00 p.m.	Free time
2.00 p.m.	Departure for home
3.00 p.m.	Stop for a snack
3.45 p.m.	Continue journey
5.00 p.m.	Arrive back at church

A different event programme

Friday

6.00 p.m.	Departure from church
7.30 p.m.	Stop for a snack
8.15 p.m.	Continue journey
9.30 p.m.	Arrive at venue and move in
10.00 p.m.	Session 1 (getting acquainted with one another, brief introduction to the theme)
11.00 p.m.	Recreation (games, singing, etc.)
Midnight	Session 2 (should emphasize interaction to hold group's attention)

Saturday

1.00 a.m.	Free time (with set limits such as indoor activities only, quiet in sleeping quarters. Games, music etc. provided, and also refreshments)

Everything after 1.00 a.m. is optional.

2.00 a.m.	Creative worship (maybe by candlelight)
3.00 a.m.	Film or video (not necessarily religious, but appropriate)
5.00 a.m.	Lights out – everyone to bed
11.00 a.m.	Brunch – a good, satisfying meal
Midday	Session 3 (continued theme development)
1.00 p.m.	Free time
5.00 p.m.	Tea
6.00 p.m.	Session 4 (continued theme development)
7.00 p.m.	Celebration time (games, sketches, maybe a talent show)
8.30 p.m.	Refreshments and free time
10.00 p.m.	Lights out

Sunday

9.00 a.m.	Breakfast
10.00 a.m.	Session 5 (theme conclusion, worship)
11.00 a.m.	Tidy up, pack up
Midday	Lunch
1.00 p.m.	Free time
2.00 p.m.	Departure for home
3.00 p.m.	Stop for a snack
3.45 p.m.	Continue journey
5.15 p.m.	Arrive back at church

Chapter 13

A selection of themes and formats

The theme of a weekend is the main topic that will be explored (for example, death and dying). Everything done and studied during the time should somehow promote a better understanding of the theme (for example, visiting a centre for terminally ill patients, listening to a hospice trainer talk about living with the knowledge that death is imminent, etc.)

Choose your theme carefully; ask your group members for suggestions. They may have a particular topic they want to learn more about.

Once you have chosen the theme, you will need to determine the format of the weekend. The format is the way the trip is put together. It's the combination of studies, activities, discussions, role plays, etc., that make up the whole event.

Since the format determines how the theme will be experienced, consider all possibilities before making your final decisions. Sometimes a film is best (for dealing with subjects that may be awkward to discuss in detail). Sometimes a special leader is best (for learning about particular topics, such as cults). And sometimes experimental activities are best (for practising self-improvement skills).

The format also influences who will attend (for example, brothers and sisters may be at a weekend focusing on siblings), where the event will be held (for example, a houseboat is a great place to study Paul's journeys) and when certain things will happen (for example, a sense of persecution may be more effective in the middle of the night). Generally, your theme will be the what and why of the weekend; your format will be the how, who, where and when.

Here are several ideas for weekend themes and formats. Imagine how they'd work in your group. Expand them or take them apart and use the pieces. Let them help you think of further ideas.

SCHOOL-LEAVER SPECIAL

Your church could honour its school leavers by giving them a unique houseparty experience – all about them! Stage a surprise *This Is Your Life* presentation for each member. Ask parents to contribute memorabilia (particularly baby pictures, favourite stuffed animal, junior school artwork and handwriting samples). Ask friends to share childhood memories. Collect as much information and material as possible and plan the programme. Parents, siblings and pets could make "unexpected" guest appearances.

MARRIAGE WEEKEND

Pair boys and girls and have a mock wedding ceremony. Hand out marriage certificates (that expire at the close of the weekend). The couples must sit together at meetings, eat together and spend free time together (but not share a room). Discuss managing budgets, assign "salaries" and instruct each couple to plan a budget; inform couples that the husband has been laid off, or the wife's £50 contact lenses broke or the dog needs an operation. Invite (real) couples to talk with your group about special joys and problems of different stages of marriage. Invite a marriage counsellor to discuss "getting along" in marriage – or show a video on the subject, e.g. *Side by Side (CPAS)*. Study scripture verses about marriage.

DECISION-MAKING WEEKEND

Take your group away to study and practise making decisions using biblical guidelines and principles. Pack the weekend with decisions that the group needs to make. You might provide food for meals but let them decide what combinations of food to eat when, who will prepare it, how, etc. Discuss biblical principles for determining what's right and what's wrong. Set up situations where the young people must make decisions – outside the cinema when friends suddenly decide to sneak in through the side door; in the classroom during a test when Sue's paper is in clear view. *Tension Getters* (also published by Bible Society) has many such situations and case studies.

CULT AWARENESS WEEKEND

Your youth group will expect to learn about cults. Teach them by using some of the methods that cults use. Determine beliefs and entice the group to join. Develop rituals and incantations, use peculiar dress, etc. "Deprogramming" (debriefing) is vital. Discuss how they felt. Help them identify the marks of the cults and list what separates cults from Christianity.

Discuss why so many young people are drawn into the cults and what can be done about it. This is an experience they'll remember.

CAMPING WEEKEND
With a leader experienced in camping, your group could leave civilization behind and head for the Lake District, a forest or a national park. Preparation is important. Study scripture passages like the Israelites wandering in the wilderness and Jesus' experience in the wilderness. Discuss the "wilderness" areas in group members' lives.

CURRENT EVENTS WEEKEND
Take your group on an adventure in exploring the difficult issues that Christians face. Have plenty of newspapers on hand and encourage the group members to identify articles that contain controversial or otherwise difficult issues. Discuss them. Find scripture verses that apply. Try to determine the responses your group would like to have (to hunger, prejudice, homosexuality, etc.).

GET-TO-KNOW-EACH-OTHER WEEKEND
Use this at the beginning of a new year with your youth group – or any time during the year when there are new members. Set aside each hour during the weekend for getting to know a person. For instance, 9 to 10 on Saturday morning could be "John Smith hour": John may tell about himself and show his rock collection or play the drums for you; his friends may add interesting details about childhood schemes; his parents may provide a letter about him for you to read to the group, as well as photographs to pass round, etc. Work with each individual ahead of time to plan his or her hour-long "presentation".

SOLO WEEKEND
Take your group to a campsite in the great outdoors during

warm weather. On the Friday evening study together the times when Jesus was alone and discuss solitude. On Saturday after breakfast send group members off with packed lunches to spend the whole day alone. They may take items with them – Bible, other books, etc. – but encourage them to experience at least one hour doing nothing but sitting on a rock and thinking about life. One caution, though: there is always the possibility of accident or other danger, so don't let the group get right out of touch. You are responsible for their safety during the weekend. When the group is back together, discuss reflections and discoveries. Then have a party to celebrate togetherness!

DEATH AND DYING WEEKEND

Visit a nursing home and talk with the residents; visit a centre for terminally ill patients and talk with them. Return to base and study Jesus' and Paul's attitudes toward death. Discuss how they compare with the attitudes your group saw in the elderly and terminally ill people. Invite a hospice nurse to talk about life before death. Go back to your site and study scripture verses about death and what happens when people die. Get a church member whose relative has died to tell the group how he or she handled the loss. Perhaps a group member who's had a family member who died would relate that experience. Get everyone to write his or her own obituary. Discuss what group members would like to be remembered for.

EXPLORING FAITHS WEEKEND

Attend a Jewish synagogue, and Christian worship of another tradition than your own; visit a mosque and other churches where you live. Discuss why there are so many different faiths, how they are alike and how they are different, what was liked about each, etc. The group may want to write their experiences in journals.

WEEKEND IN THE FUTURE

The year is 2025. Everyone should wear clothes from "2025 Designers". Use food colouring to turn milk, mashed potatoes etc., into odd foods of the future. Create a special language ("What-yips are-sug you-yips thinking-sug?"). Discuss future subjects: knowing God's will, choosing a career/college/job, living with the threat of nuclear war, etc. Get group members to write their autobiographies through to the year 2025 and discuss them.

HOW-TO-HELP WEEKEND
Get an instructor to train your group in basic first aid procedures. Role play situations where group members help others. Study Jesus' ministry of healing people both physically and spiritually.

PERSECUTION WEEKEND
Group members pretend they are first-century Christians who are experiencing persecution or twentieth-century Christians who are forced to worship secretly. Take everyone camping. The group must move secretively and quietly or risk being discovered. Study the actual persecutions of the early Christians and the present-day troubles of Christians in many countries. Tell Corrie ten Boom's story. Arrange for a couple of church members to "discover" your group dramatically during the night and threaten torture, yet allow everyone to "escape" safely to a predetermined hiding place. At dawn, return to the campsite for more rest. After breakfast, discuss how Christians now can prepare for possible times of persecution (for example, by reading their Bibles, developing good prayer habits, worshipping in homes as well as the church, etc.).

CAREER WEEKEND
Get church members from a variety of occupations to give presentations to your group about their work – including what they like most about it and what they like least. Encourage the group to ask questions. You may be able to get aptitude tests from school careers advisors that can help determine what professions your group members are best suited for. Provide materials on a variety of vocations and encourage young people to consider seriously which they will choose. Discuss strategies for achieving career goals. This activity might work best in consultation with the local schools careers service, which might be able to give valuable help and advice.

VIDEO WEEKEND

Take some video recording equipment and have some fun. Your group could role play and videotape situations that could serve as discussion starters for the church members or other youth groups. Brainstorm and produce commercials for Christianity. Take your equipment to a street corner near your church. Interview people on the street. Ask them what they think about God, nuclear weapons, assemblies in schools or some other topic of concern for your church. Get your group to stage a full production and videotape it. The options are endless – and the learning is fun.

DRUG AWARENESS WEEKEND

Invite a special leader to talk to your group about drug use and abuse. Help the young people learn how to recognize when their friends are abusing drugs and need help. Discuss why people take drugs and what Christianity can offer them. Role play talking with such friends and offering them help. Discuss how young people can try to convince friends to stop abusing drugs. Discuss a story or show a film about a person who was once addicted to drugs but isn't any more.

FUNDRAISING WEEKEND

Devote a weekend to fundraising – planning and doing. Use a posterboard calendar of the coming year to help your group pin-point the events for which they need to raise money. Brainstorm ideas for raising the money and choose the ones the group will do. Plan the projects as much as possible. For a half day of this trip your group could run a car wash or other basic fundraiser.

POVERTY AWARENESS WEEKEND

Take your group to a depressed inner city or "run down" area. Fast for 24 hours. Separate the young people into pairs to visit people and offer services to them (cleaning, repair work, etc.). Visit a local church, soup kitchen, community centre or rescue mission. Discuss experiences; what did the group "hear" when they listened to the people they were with? Have an in-depth Bible study on Jesus' ministry to the poor and his instructions about caring for them. Resolve to serve the area in the future by sending money or clothes or by doing work projects. This kind of activity would work best in co-operation with a welfare or mission organization already involved in the area.

PARABLE WEEKEND

Explore the meaning of Jesus' parables with your group. Act them out. Discuss for each what Jesus was trying to say to his listeners then and what the parable can say to people now. Create a modern version of a parable, as though Jesus were telling it today, and act it out. Is the meaning easier to see in the new version? You might also talk with your group about some of the background information on the parables.

FILM FESTIVAL

Get away with your group for a weekend of good films. Don't limit yourself to films from Christian producers. Discuss the films' meanings and implications from a biblical perspective.

CONFIRMATION WEEKEND

For those young people about to be confirmed or take church membership, a special weekend of fun and review. The leader gives an overview of the lessons that led to their readiness for confirmation. Plenty of fun and games will help build unity and a sense of community as they prepare for this important event.

LEADERSHIP DEVELOPMENT WEEKEND

Here's a chance to discover the leadership potential and abilities in your young people. Let them lead sessions on what they're good at. You may have a potpourri of topics – from how to start a stamp collection to how to say a few phrases in German. Some may prefer to lead discussions of familiar Bible passages. Work with each person ahead of time to help him or her determine a topic. The experience of leadership is what's important. Invite a speaker on leadership. Give the group a project to do (for example, list reasons why parents should give teenagers more or less responsibility) and assign a leader. Give small groups projects to do (for example, build a campfire) and don't assign leaders; watch for natural leaders to emerge. Study the leaders God used in the Bible and point out that some (like Moses) did not consider themselves as having "outgoing" personalities, yet God accomplished great things through them.

BROTHERS AND SISTERS WEEKEND

Siblings of youth group members attend this trip as well. Plan activities that require brothers and sisters to work together on tasks – and experience a mutual sense of achievement. For example get siblings to describe or act out something unique about their family life for the rest of the group. Get the group to discuss problems that arise in sibling relationships, suggest possible ways of handling the problems and role play the suggestions. Study siblings' conflicts in the Bible (for example, Cain and Abel, Mary and Martha) and determine whether they were properly resolved. Study scripture passages about the unity among Christians as the children of God. If the group includes younger children, allow plenty of time for developing relationships by playing games.

LAW AND ORDER WEEKEND

Arrange with your local police in advance to let your youth group visit the local police station. Study the penal system and invite an officer from your local police to talk to the group. You might stage an "arrest" during one of the preparatory sessions (searches, "booking", fingerprinting and mug shots are all part of the experience). Debriefing the group afterwards is important. Discuss what happened and how everyone felt about it. Study what the Bible says about justice.

ADVENTURE WEEKEND

Take a risk! Encourage your group to go rafting, rock climbing, or camping. Or challenge them to climb a 14-foot wall, walk balance beams, work out how to get all the group members on to a three-foot-square platform – or over a five-foot-high taut rope without touching it. What about an army assault course? The young people will enjoy the support from other group members and the sense of accomplishment. Study scripture verses about overcoming fear. Discuss building community and the importance of Christian community.

PLANNING WEEKEND

Do you get frustrated planning your programmes for your group at the last minute? Is it a hassle getting people to look ahead and take responsibility for some aspect of your group's life and spiritual growth?

A planning weekend might be just what you need to help you determine your purpose, to identify your focus clearly for the next few months or a year.

Identify the people you feel should be involved. Do you have elected officers or coordinators? If so, they would be a core. Others might be invited as well. Sometimes the whole group can be involved in planning ahead for the year.

Some possible questions for group focus during the trip:

- The purposes of our group are...
- Next year I feel our group needs to...
- God seems to be telling us to...
- One of the prime opportunities we have is...

These open-ended questions can lead to input and goal statements that can then be specifically translated into programme ideas and suggestions. The weekend can even include scheduling of future events and the division of labour for implementing them.

SIMULATION GAME WEEKEND
Encourage your group to create a simulation game that you would live/play for a whole day or weekend. The book *Everyone's a Winner* (Bible Society) will help you see how you can create your own exciting simulation games.

ACTION WEEKEND
Does your church have special mission projects which your group might serve? Do you live near a large city that has community centres, or special programmes for youth, adults, elderly citizens?

Do you have any special concentrations of people near you – a retirement home, a treatment centre for alcoholics, a hospital, a child-care centre, or psychiatric hospital? If so, you have a unique opportunity for Christian action and involvement. Get your group to make a list of such institutions and organizations. Do Bible studies on some of the following scriptures: 1 John 2.5 and 4.16–21; John 13.34–35; Matthew 5.43–48 and 25.37–41; 2 Corinthians 5.17–18; Luke 4.16–21; and Ephesians 5.16–17.

Get someone to contact several of the organizations to find out what kind of involvement they might appreciate. Encourage the group to select one. You could contact them and arrange to work together for a day, a weekend or a week. Experience the joy of learning to be Christ's reconcilers and healers!

TRAVEL WEEKEND

Do you have a yearning to see the world, to go to new and distant places? There are lots of ways to travel. Determine the cost you can afford for the weekend and then work out how far you can go on that amount of money. The possibilities are endless, and the fun and creativity in stretching the pounds is fantastic.

Bike it. The bicycle has been reckoned to be the most efficient and ecologically sound means of transport ever devised.

Form a road show. Your group, large or small, could create a 20- or 30-minute programme to share with other groups along the way. Write to other churches and arrange to sleep in their church halls and to perform for them. Great fun, and a good way to make new friends. You don't have to be professional actors. One group started with the well-known theme "Happiness is..." and created 20-second scenes illustrating the different ideas, plus many that they thought up on their own. These were interspersed with appropriate short scripture readings, poetry and other creations from the group.

DISCOVERING YOUR COMMUNITY

A home weekend can give you new eyes to see your neighbours. Send out several people with cameras to photograph parts of your community that few people ever see.

Arrange for 15-minute interviews with several members of the community – a policeman, a barber or hairdresser, a business-person, a welfare worker, a lawyer, a doctor, a union leader, a farmer, the mayor, a school governor, a newspaper reporter, etc. Ask them these three questions, record their answers on a cassette tape recorder and take notes:

1. What do you see to be the genuine strengths and assets of our community?
2. What do you see to be the needs or problem issues that face our community?

3. What can the Christian community do to be part of the solutions to our community's problems, from your perspective?

Map your community. Ask members of the group, using crayons, to draw your community as they see it – significant groups, structures, "dividing lines", etc.

Do a newspaper collage. Create a collage from back issues of the local paper showing strength and problem areas.

The information gathered can be the basis for continuing discussion and reflection on your opportunities as Christians to influence the communities in which you live as ministers and servants of Jesus Christ. The pain/problem areas can be listed during the report time. These could be put in order of priority and one selected for possible group action.

The information might be the focus for a special reporting session to the whole congregation regarding what you have learnt and what opportunities you have to love the people God has created.

MULTI-CULTURAL EXTRAVAGANZA
Do people from other racial or ethnic backgrounds share your community? Possibly many different heritages? Even if it is only one, you can have fun finding out more about each other and experiencing what it would be like to be part of that culture.

Plan the weekend to include the foods, the folklore, the history, the dances, the games and the religious heritage of the cultures in your community. (Maybe the other cultures are non-Christian. This will give you an opportunity to share your faith with them). If there are multi-cultural churches nearby, get in touch and work together in joint planning.

PART TWO

PROGRAMMES FOR YOUTH GROUP EVENTS

Programme 1

Cliques

One of the most potentially destructive forces in youth work is the clique. Cliques offer a teenager a place to belong and a sense of security. However, they also cause the exclusion of a great number of people, hinder interaction and stifle outreach.

This weekend provides a group with an opportunity to see how cliques develop, what it's like to be on the wrong side of a clique, how God feels about cliques, and what we can do about them.

Before the weekend

1. Issue a list of things the group will need to bring. Don't forget to include Bible, notebook and pen.
2. Collect permission slips and any monies owed before you leave to avoid confusion when you arrive.
3. Assign people to pray specifically for each group member while on the retreat. In the past we have enlisted people both to pray and to write a note of encouragement to their assigned young person which we passed on at our Sunday morning meeting.
4. Read through the sessions to familiarize yourself with the topics. Get together materials needed to be printed or assembled:

    ☐ Songs for Friday evening.
    ☐ Chairs arranged for the first meeting.
    ☐ Props for *Go Away* (page 71) for the second meeting.
    ☐ Copies of *English Test* (page 75) for the second meeting – one per person.
    ☐ Props for *Foto Match* (page 76) for the third meeting.
    ☐ Copies of *Autograph Hunt* (page 79) for the fourth meeting – one per person.

Also get ready: overhead projector, screen, video (see Friday evening notes), snack foods.

While on the way

If possible plan interaction games or activities to get the group better acquainted and comfortably talking and sharing together while travelling to the weekend centre.

Either while travelling or as soon as you arrive (it can't be done ahead because of absentees or last-minute attenders) get a core of your adult leaders together to divide the young people into small groups for the weekend. Participants will stay in their groups during meetings, for free time, team games, cleaning up, meal sittings etc. These groups are essential to the weekend's success. Try to get a good balance in each group between popular people, shy ones, talkers, disrupters, the spiritually mature, and athletes (for team games). You should also separate as much as possible any existing or potential cliques you might already have. Your groups should consist of six to ten people. Seven to nine is ideal.

Once this is done, place your leaders in these groups to be responsible for facilitating sharing, group identity and spirit. Discuss with your leaders who would work best with which group.

Weekend devotions

Get the entire group together to give them their assigned reading, questions to think about and directed prayer for Saturday and Sunday. If the weather permits, let them find a place outside alone to do their devotions.

SATURDAY DEVOTIONS

1. Read John 13.34–35. What does this say to you about love?
2. Read James 2.1–9. What does this say to you about love? Do you ever find yourself doing this?
3. Pray for yourself, to be open this weekend to God and to each other. Pray the same way for the others in your group.

SUNDAY DEVOTIONS

1. Read Colossians 3.12–14. How well do you exhibit these qualities?
2. Read Matthew 13.1–8. What kind of people do these seeds represent?

3. Pray for yourself, to be open and to take home and put into practice what you have learnt. Pray the same for the others in your group.

Programme for the weekend

Friday evening
After unpacking get everyone together for Friday evening's activities.

1. It is important that you go over your own particular ground rules with the young people right away.
2. Go over the plan and purpose of the weekend. Put copies in the eating areas and other key places.
3. After dividing the young people into teams for the weekend, do a song search in the dark. Give each member of a given team the title of the same familiar song on a slip of paper. Do the same thing for each team using different songs for each team. Instruct them not to let anyone else see their paper. When the lights go out they are to start humming their song and finding others of the same song. Tell them how many others there will be. The first team to finish gets a reward – first sitting for breakfast, etc.
4. Show a video.
5. Group singing or lights out, depending on the time.

Saturday morning (1½ hours). What is a clique?

1. Open with prayer.
2. Play *Untangle*. Organize everyone into their groups and get them to stand in a circle. Everyone grabs hands with others not next to them and without letting go, gets himself back into a circle all untangled and still joining hands. Mention that the first group to finish gets a prize – first to have lunch, etc.
3. Read John 13.34–35.
4. Announce the weekend topic – cliques, what causes them, how God feels about them, what you can do about them.
5. Ask everyone to define and discuss the meaning of a clique,

then read the following definition: "A clique is a small exclusive circle of people who have common interests. Once formed, there is an unwillingness by members of the group to admit others into their circle of friendship."

6. Form groups and ask each group to:

   a. do a play or sketch
   b. write a song
   c. write a poem or story about a clique – real or imagined, but typical of cliques

   Vote on the best.

7. Explain and discuss the following types of cliques:

   Style/fashion followers – very popular with popular people. They feel others are inferior. Very judgemental.

   Rowdies – love to cause trouble and pick on and make fun of others. Spend a lot of time telling others how rowdy they are.

   Super spirituals – proud of being "good Christians" (not doing certain things, knowing the Bible etc.). Talk about how good they are and how bad others are. Look down on those who are less "perfect".

   Just averages – held together by need for survival. They are usually bitter and resentful, or awestruck by the other cliques.

   We sing or play in the band together – talented people whose whole life is built around singing or playing music. They are so busy they don't have time for anyone else.

   Me and my girlfriend and my friend and his girlfriend – they are easy to spot: they look welded together! All conversation revolves around Saturday's date (past, present, and future). Always looking at each other. No time for anyone else.

   The athletes – small but powerful group. They hang together because of athletic "greatness" which makes them feel above others. They love to talk about sports and have macho contests.

Ask the young people to come up with any others if they can.

8. Before the session, arrange the chairs and tell the group as they come in that the chairs are not to be moved. This is how the chairs should be set up, and the people they represent:

   a. A group of chairs in a circle all linked together: the group of regular teens who attend the youth group.
   b. A chair in the middle of the circle: the person who wants to be the centre of attention.
   c. A few chairs outside the group: visitors to the youth group who can't seem to break through and be a part of the group in the circle.
   d. A chair next to the door: a new person who has just entered the group.
   e. A chair outside the door, looking in: someone wanting to enter the youth group but who is afraid to come in.
   f. A chair on top of the table: a person who criticizes and looks down on everyone else.
   g. A broken chair or a chair that's different from all the others: a person in the group who may be a little different from the rest because of a handicap, a foreign accent, etc.
   h. A small cluster of three or four chairs apart from the large circle: that group of people who stick together and won't let anyone into their group.

You can probably think of some other ways to represent various groupings within a group, and you should try to arrange it so that everyone has a chair, and there are no chairs left over. As the group arrives, give each person a number at random and instruct him/her to sit in the chair that has the same number. During the meeting have a discussion on cliques using the following questions. Everyone must stay in the seats that they have been assigned during the entire meeting.

9. Questions for discussion:

   a. How can cliques be helpful?
   b. How can cliques be harmful?
   c. Why are some people not included in a clique?

10. Some closing comments: point out that your youth group doesn't necessarily have a clique problem but we all have cliquish tendencies. This topic is being considered because:

   a. Cliquish tendencies can lead to some bad things if not nipped in the bud.
   b. It will help everyone deal better with cliques at school.

   Ask the following questions, to be answered silently. (A "yes" answer to any of these means the weekend will be helpful to the group.)

   ☐ Do you ever catch yourself feeling that you and your friends are more "with it" than others in the youth group?
   ☐ Do you ever try to discourage someone from being involved with you and your friends because they wouldn't fit the mould of what's acceptable to your group?
   ☐ If you are talking to someone and one of your close friends comes into the room do you immediately leave that person and go to talk to your friend?
   ☐ Do you make it a point to get to know new people at our youth meetings?

11. Close in prayer.

Saturday afternoon (1½ hours). What causes cliques?

1. Open with prayer.
2. Play *Squat*. Get each team to form a circle facing the same direction. On the count of three everyone sits down on the knees of the person behind them. Then do it as a total group, combining all the teams into one big circle. (Needs a large area.)
3. Play *Go Away*, a clique simulation game. The following materials are needed: toothpicks, glue, old magazines, clay and poster board for each team.
   Divide into groups. Explain that each team uses the supplies and works together to construct a symbol of what "community" or "togetherness" means to them. Tell each group to be

prepared to explain its completed symbol and set a time limit.

The "sting": Before this session, for each team pick one person who is to argue, refuse to cooperate, hinder progress and otherwise be a headache. Caution the "plants" not to make their misbehaviour too obvious. Explain that their purpose is to test the teams' reactions to negative behaviour. Locate the teams far enough apart so they can't see each other.

After the teams have worked on the project long enough for the "plant" to cause some problems, stop the activity temporarily.

Explain that you're also trying an experiment to see if a new team can catch up with the existing teams. Explain that you'll form the new team by taking one person from each existing team. Tell each team to send one person from their membership to the new team. Normally, each team will send the troublemaker, but even if someone else is sent, it doesn't change the experience.

Under the guise of giving the new team "catch-up" instructions, explain that in a minute or two each person is to return to his original team and ask to be readmitted, saying he doesn't like the new group.

When each team has had enough time to react, either by accepting the person or by refusing readmittance, stop the activity and call all the groups back together. It's a good idea to confess that each group had a "plant".

Use some or all of the following questions:

- How did you feel about the "plant" in your team?
- How did you feel about having to tell one person to leave?
- Why did you reject the person you did?
- How did you feel when they returned and asked to be readmitted?
- If you didn't accept them, what were your reasons?
- If you accepted them again, why? Did you make any conditions for rejoining the group?
- How did you show you really accepted them again?

- How did the "plants" feel about the whole process?
- In what ways was this experience similar to the way groups treat some people at school or church?
- How do most "real" groups deal with someone who's different?

You could end this experience by getting everyone to help plan a session where the emphasis is on learning how to accept people who are new to the group.

During one of your meetings send one of the young people on a short errand. While he or she is gone, lead the rest of the group in a game that requires total participation of all members so that the latecomer couldn't possibly play. Also, instruct the group to ignore the "errand person" when he or she returns. After the game, discuss with the "misfit" his or her feelings about being left out. Get the group to reflect on a time when they were newcomers and ask each to share a one-word description of what it felt like. You might then read John 8.1–11 about the woman caught in adultery, and discuss Jesus' gentle attitude. Role play what might have happened the next day as the woman runs into two friends. Conclude with the following role play: a visitor walks into one of your weekly youth meetings. Repeat the role play several times until the group know how to treat visitors.

4. Discuss the reasons for cliques:

   a. Prideful status seeking. As human beings we have a sinful nature, a big part of which is pride.

      Pride tells us that we must be the centre of attention, so we deceive ourselves into thinking that climbing into a higher status group will make us happier. We tend to use people.

      Jesus was not a status seeker! He was more concerned with what God wanted him to do than with who accepted him.

      Read Romans 12.14–16 and Matthew 9.9–13. Discuss why Jesus was not a status seeker. What can we learn from him?

   b. Fear and insecurity. We all have a desire to be and feel

needed and wanted.

The problem is that we look too much to our friends to meet that need. The last thing we want to lose is our importance and favour with our friends.

Because we don't usually love ourselves and have low self-esteem and aren't secure in our specialness to God and others, we tend to shut out newcomers because they might threaten our position in the group. We put our security in people and not in God.

Read Isaiah 31.1–3, Proverbs 3.5–6 and 1 John 4.18–19.

c. Selfishness and laziness. Invite the group to do the English test on the following page.

Read the following instructions and pass out the test.

"Mark this paragraph into sentences using capitals at the beginning of sentences, full stops at the end, and commas, etc. where needed. Once begun, do not go back and try to correct."

As with the English test we judge too many things from our own perspective and are too lazy to check things out first. We do the same with people. We have prejudices and form opinions too soon and too easily without getting to know them. This is where we usually struggle most.

Once we reach a place where we have a close-knit group of friends it is easy to become indifferent to others. We feel we no longer need to reach out to someone who needs us as a friend. We are very content where we are. We all know how much easier it is just to be with our close friends. Making new friends is work. This is selfish and lazy.

God has something to say about this. Read Matthew 5.43–47. Just loving our friends is no great deed of love. We need to go beyond that.

5. Close with prayer.

Saturday evening (1 hour). Why God opposes cliques

1. Open with prayer.
2. In their groups get each person to team up with a partner. Get them to play *Mimic*. Each one sees how well he can mirror or copy the other's actions, speech, expressions. Each

---

English test

He is a young man yet experienced in vice and wickedness he is never found in opposing the works of iniquity he takes delight in the downfall of his neighbours he never rejoices in the prosperity of his fellow creatures he is always ready to assist in destroying the peace of society he takes no pleasure in serving the Lord he is uncommonly diligent in sowing discord among his friends and acquaintances he takes no pride in labouring to promote the cause of Christianity he has not been negligent in endeavouring to tear down the church he makes no effort to subdue his evil passions he strives hard to build up Satan's kingdom he lends no aid to the support of the gospel in mission he contributes largely to the devil he will never go to heaven he must go where he will receive his just reward.

How the English test should be corrected

He is a young man, yet experienced. In vice and wickedness he is never found. In opposing the works of iniquity he takes delight. In the downfall of his neighbours he never rejoices. In the prosperity of his fellow creatures he is always ready to assist. In destroying the peace of society he takes no pleasure. In serving the Lord he is uncommonly diligent. In sowing discord among his friends and acquaintances he takes no pride. In labouring to promote the cause of Christianity he has not been negligent. In endeavouring to tear down the church he makes no effort. To subdue his evil passions he tries hard. To build up Satan's kingdom he lends no aid. To the support of the gospel in mission he contributes largely. To the devil he will never go. To heaven he must go, where he will receive his just reward.

---

group picks its best pair to mimic before the whole group to see which pair is best of all.

3. Why God opposes cliques (discussion):

   a. Cliques go against the fairness of God. Read Ephesians 5.1–2. As with the game *Mimic* we are to imitate our Father perfectly in all things, but we can mimic our Father enough so that others should be able to tell whose children we are.

Here are some things about God we should mimic.

- **God's impartiality.** Read Deuteronomy 10.16–19. Looks, wealth, fame, heritage, get no special treatment from God. We should treat all people the same.
- **God's love.** God is not only impartial, he loves all people too. Not just in words or ideas but with action!

Read Philippians 2.5–8. God had every right to dissociate himself totally from us. But Jesus left his rightful status and came to earth for us. We should follow Jesus' example. Read 1 John 3.16. This is love with action!

b. Do *Foto Match* (see below) to illustrate the following reason before giving it:

Cliques cause us to show favouritism to others on faulty, shallow grounds.

Doing *Foto Match* shows us how we form strong opinions on appearance alone. Our first impression was exaggerated yet we all do it to a degree. Read James 2.1-19. God is fair. He shows no favouritism. Read Luke 10.25–37.

Foto Match

Hang up 20 or so photos of people (all kinds – old, young, black, white, attractive, ugly, fat, slim, wealthy, poor, etc.). Get the group to write descriptions of each person based on what they see in the picture. Collect them all and combine all the individual descriptions into a list which accurately reflects the group consensus. Attach the descriptions to each photo. Then answer the following questions:

- Choose five you'd like to get to know. Why did you choose those five?
- Is there any one person you would not want anything to do with? Why?
- Who, if any, would you be willing to marry?
- If you and only five other people were to be allowed to live and everyone else were to be executed, which five would be chosen? Why?

No doubt each of us knows people who are not naturally attractive to us. However, these people have emotional and spiritual needs and pains too. God does not want us to hurt these people further through a spirit of excluding them. But he wants us to reach out to them and express compassion in meeting their needs.

No one can be rejected by a group for very long before they begin to realize that they are being rejected. This often results in a negative response from the person being "put off". Not only is this divisive to the Body of Christ, but it may seriously hinder that person's growth in Christ. Paul warned the Galatian Christians: read Galatians 5.14–15.

Such backbiting and "devouring" is just what Satan wants to happen. Nothing could please him more. But God wants us to build one another up, to encourage each other. As Romans 13.10 states, "If you love someone, you will never do him wrong; to love, then, is to obey the whole Law".

Jesus taught that one of the most powerful ways in which a person is attracted to him is the love that he sees between Christians. In John 13.34–35 he said, "And now I give you a new commandment: love one another. As I have loved you, so you must love one another. If you have love for one another, then everyone will know that you are my disciples."

It is sad when outsiders come to our group seeking love, and find that because of our disobedience, fear, insecurity, laziness, selfishness and pride, we act just like the very people who have hurt them. These people look at our actions to see if there is living proof that Christ is real. If, on the one hand, we say that Christ gives us love, and on the other hand, we do not practise love, but rather are cliquish and cruel, we are living a lie.

4. Closing comments. Watch for little ways we might do any of these things we've discussed. It's very easy to forget and get lazy and comfortable with our close friends. It's normal to be afraid to reach out. We all do these things. If you do:

a. Confess your faults.
b. As an act of faith, show love to those outside your

group. When you do, it will get easier and more fulfill-
ing.
c. Be the initiator in reaching out and in telling your
friends to reach out. If you have been shut out by a
clique, this can be a time of growth and understanding.
Being left out of a group can draw you closer to God if
you let it. Don't be bitter, angry or feel sorry for yourself.
That's really more important.

5. Close in prayer.

**Sunday morning (1½ hours). How to be a clique-breaker –
what can we do?**

1. Open with prayer.
2. Play *Autograph Hunt* (see next page). The first person to get
the necessary signatures wins.
3. Discussion: being a clique breaker also involves change.
Read Colossians 3.12–14. It involves changing from what's
natural! (See verse 10.) Get the group to come up with what
these words mean in relation to breaking cliques: compassion, kindness, humility, gentleness, patience, tolerance,
forgiveness.
All these are very similar to the fruit of the Spirit (Galatians
5.22–26). They are all also very important in being a servant
– the key to friendship.
Read Colossians 3.12–14 concerning love.
4. Close with prayer.

Sunday afternoon (1½–2 hours). Above all, love

1. Open with prayer.
2. Read Colossians 3.12–14. Explain that "change" needs
action. We are not just to talk about or think about being
compassionate, kind, gentle, patient and loving. We are to
act these ways.
3. Read John 13.34–35. Discuss how "everyone will know".
What are some ways?
4. Read 1 John 3.18. Directions: get your group to form a circle
and put one person in the middle of the circle. Starting with
the adult group leader, go round the circle, each member

AUTOGRAPH HUNT

Someone who uses mouth-wash regularly	Someone with 2 brothers	Someone with blond hair at least 12 in. long	Someone who plays football	Someone who has been abroad
Someone who owns a dog	Someone who is wearing con-tact lenses	Someone who plays chess a lot	Someone who can touch his palms to the floor	Someone who owns a motor cycle
Someone with red hair	Someone who watches soap operas	Sign your own name	Someone who got an A in English	Someone who has touched a snake
Someone who has been to Scotland	Someone who weighs over 10 stone	Someone who reads comic books	Someone who has met some-one famous	Someone who ate at McDonalds this week
Someone who's never changed a nappy	Someone who weighs under 7 stone	Someone who owns a horse	Someone wear-ing blue socks	Someone who can say all the books of the Bible

non-verbally expressing his love and care for that person. When you've gone all the way around, put the next person in the middle and repeat this process until everyone has been in the centre. Examples of non-verbal expression are a hug, a touch, a look, giving a gift. Be creative! Be genuine!

5.   Get back in one large group and share how this went. Was it hard to do? Would it have been easier to do verbally? How did you feel receiving? Giving? Which was harder?

6.   Give the group the following challenge: "How will you, as individuals and as a group, reach outside this youth group to share with others in need of Christ and fellowship and friendship?"

7.   Get them back in their groups and let them brainstorm about the following points. Pick one target person whom their group will reach out to.

Who will it be? A person from the church but not very involved, or a person from school they all know? (If your situation involves many people from many different schools and they can't come up with one person, adapt this and get them to divide up into minigroups within the groups; they will have to do the best they can at picking several target people. You may want to divide up the groups beforehand so this problem can be avoided.)

What will you do? Examples: invite them to church or youth group; have lunch with them at school; say hello to them every day as a starter; call them on the phone; invite them to do something with you or your friends. Be creative! Develop a plan.

As a group pray for this person. The more you pray for someone the more you'll care and be concerned for them. This really requires you to be a servant just as Jesus was.

8.   Get them back into one large group and share together their results group by group.

9.   Close with prayer.

Programme 2

God's bod

The theme of this event is that God asks his children to dedicate their bodies to him.

Preparation

The leadership meet to discuss responsibilities for various portions of the weekend.

A suggestion for a pre-weekend session:

1. Find a cosy place for this session and invite all parents and youth to it. The atmosphere should be conducive to discussion, with movable chairs, soft lighting, comfortable surroundings.
2. When everyone arrives do some warm-up activities.
3. Introduce the weekend's theme and goals. Outline the entire weekend briefly and allow for questions.
4. If time permits, do part of the "Agree/Disagree" exercise (pages 90–91) with this group, allowing the parents to participate in an activity that the group will experience during the weekend.
5. Finish with refreshments.

Materials, equipment, facilities

Many conference centres have these items on hand for you to use, but it is wise to check with them beforehand.

- Some of your group's favourite songbooks.
- A video recorder.
- Some good, fun entertainment films (you could bring some with you).
- Copies of devotional booklets for group and personal use.
- Tape player with cassettes of some specially chosen music.
- Bibles, dictionaries, pencils, paper.
- Overhead projector with transparencies and pens (or large sheets of paper to put on the wall).

Friday evening

1. If you go as a group make sure you leave in time to arrive at the centre by 6.30 p.m. Unpack, assign rooms and let everyone settle in a little. Meet together as a group by 7 p.m.
Meet in a large comfortable room with movable chairs. Sit on the floor if you like. Sing some fast and fun songs to start things off.

2 7.30 p.m. – start with a warm-up exercise geared to the theme of the weekend. Good ones to try are numbers 15 or 16 from *Power Pack*, Book 1, or number 21 from *Power Pack*, Book 2. Details of these can be found in the Reading List on page 150. Emphasize that the rest of the weekend will be geared to helping people look seriously at being all that God wants them to be. Then share the weekend goals and the key verse.
End this time in prayer. Give some free time after this event.

3. 10 p.m. – it's time for a video marathon with some oldies but goodies. These could be a variety of comedies, mysteries, or dramas that the group like.

Saturday morning

1. 8 a.m. – breakfast.
2. 8.45 a.m. – small group devotions. Divide into groups of 10, with at least one leader for each group.
3. Everyone meets together for the general session at 9.30 a.m. Begin by singing fun songs for ten minutes or so. The leader then introduces the theme of the day by reading Romans 12.1–2 and saying something like this: "We are going to spend time looking at three different pressures we feel. We will move in round-robin fashion to different stands. Each stand covers the same subject all three times we rotate, so don't stay at the same stand twice. One subject is 'the effects of music'. The second topic is 'the effects of TV and the media'. The third topic covers 'peer pressure'. Each period is 40 minutes long. There'll be a five-minute break between sessions. Let's break up our group into thirds and proceed."
If leaders are scarce for these sessions, teach the entire group all three sessions, one at a time.

If you use the stand approach, here is a suggested schedule:

9.30 – 9.40	Introduction
9.45 – 10.25	First round
10.30 – 11.10	Second round
11.15 – 11.55	Third round

STAND ONE: THE EFFECTS OF MUSIC, "GETTING ROCKED WITHOUT GETTING STONED"

1. Put the following statements on the board or as graffiti around the room. Get the young people to react to each one:

   - Rock music has more suggestive lyrics than other forms of music (pop, country, opera).
   - Some rock songs have important social messages.
   - Rock music has an effect on how you behave.
   - The beat in rock music is Satanic.
   - Smashing up rock music records make an effective statement to society.
   - Christian rock is a good alternative to secular rock music.
   - It is easier to commit sexual sin on a date when you're listening to sexy music together.

2. Invite people to read the following passages and discuss how they apply to rock music: 2 Corinthians 10.5; 11.3; Philippians 4.8. (Two of these state that your mind can be led away from Christ. The question is whether or not rock music can have an effect on your mind.)

3. Pass out music evaluation sheets (see next page) and pencils. Play a secular rock song with suggestive lyrics and ask each person to evaluate it. Then discuss it. Do the same with a rock song that has meaningful/constructive lyrics. Then play a Christian rock song and evaluate it as well. Make the effort to bring a good stereo system.

   You may want to type the lyrics to the songs so that people can read them as the song plays.

4. Tell the group about a few rock musicians who have gone from secular to Christian rock.

5. Close in prayer.

Music evaluation sheet

Name of song:_____

Artist: _____

                                                    Terrible   Great
Quality of music (excluding lyrics) – Circle one: 1   2   3   4   5

Message of the song (state briefly): _____

_____

                                        Terrible   Great
Quality of the message: 1   2   3   4   5

                                        Terrible   Great
Overall quality of song: 1   2   3   4   5

Is this song worth listening to? ____Why or why not?_____

_____

STAND TWO: THE EFFECTS OF TV AND THE MEDIA

Get people to discuss the following questions.

1. Where is the television set in your home? The centre of the living room? In the kitchen? What does the location of your TV tell you about its importance to your family?
2. How many hours of TV do you watch each week?
3. What are your favourite programmes? What makes them your favourites?
4. How does TV deal with issues of morality? Does TV generally stay away from issues of right or wrong?
5. Have you ever turned a TV programme off? If so, why?
6. How would your life be different if you didn't watch TV for 30 days?
7. What are guidelines for TV watching?

STAND THREE: PEER PRESSURE

Give a copy of the *Peer Pressure or Support Group* sheet (opposite) to each person. Take 10 minutes to conduct the interviews. Discuss the findings in groups of five.

Peer pressure or support group

1. What do you think is the biggest influence on students' actions in your school?
2. If Christians don't take a stand in your school, why do you think they don't?
3. How would you define peer pressure?
4. Do parents experience peer pressure?
5. Is there a strong group pressure among Christians? Should there be?

Use a flip chart or overhead projector to tabulate the survey results. Explain that standards are important – a person needs to establish personal standards.

Tell everyone to divide the back of their survey sheets into three columns, with these headings:

PHYSICAL STANDARDS   SPIRITUAL STANDARDS   SOCIAL STANDARDS

Get everyone to read and paraphrase the following passages and fit them into one or more of the three columns. The passages are Psalm 37.1–6; Proverbs 29.25; Romans 12.1–2; Hebrews 10.24–25; and 1 John 2.15–17. For example, the Proverbs passage might fit into the social and physical standards columns.

Spend the last few minutes sharing some of the findings. Conclude with everyone vowing to support actively at least one other person in the group. End in prayer.

Saturday afternoon
Spend most of this time as organized free time.

Saturday evening

1. Dinner at 5.30 p.m. with free time afterwards.
2. 6.30 p.m. – group singing and games.
3. 7 p.m. onwards – start by saying: "We have discussed today the topic of pressure: TV, music, friends. Tonight, we'll take a look at different types of pressure. Let's read Romans 12.1–2 again, this time as a group. We have another series of sessions, only they are 30 minutes in length. Choose two of the three to attend." The schedule looks like this:

7.15 – 7.45   First round
7.50 – 8.20   Second round
8.25 – 9.30   General session

The sessions are:

- Dating and relating to others
- Loving yourself and liking it
- Friendships and their effect on you

Give directions on where to find each option. Below is an agenda for each of the three. The general session follows.

OPTION ONE: DATING AND RELATING TO OTHERS
Give each person a copy of *Making Your Dating Life Count* (see below). Split everyone into groups of three and let them work on this material for 20 minutes. Discuss everyone's findings.

OPTION TWO: LOVING YOURSELF AND LIKING IT
Hand out *Liking Yourself* sheets (see opposite) and get everyone to complete their copy on their own.

After all have finished, discuss their feelings. How important do they feel? How important does God feel they are? Comment that in God's eyes we are objects of great value. Follow this outline:

Making your dating life count

Work through this exercise with two other people.
Read Ecclesiastes 11.7–12.1.

1. Look up the word "perspective" in the dictionary and write down what it means.
2. How would you define "spiritual perspective"?
3. Write Ecclesiastes 11.7–8 in your own words.
4. How should you "enjoy your youth" according to verse 9?
5. Does "God is going to judge you for whatever you do" scare you? Why?
6. How can you follow Ecclesiastes 12.1?
7. Read 1 Peter 4.1–5. How should you act as a responsible person towards others according to this passage?
   How does this passage apply to dating?

Liking yourself

How do you feel about yourself? Who are *You*? What is your identity? Have you ever been aware of your "self" at any given time? This is called by another name: our self-concept. It is the image we have of ourselves, or our mental picture of ourselves. Three questions define who we are:

Who am I?
What am I?
Why am I?

Who am I: I am a male or female. I am _____ years old. This is my identity as a person.

What am I: I am a: housewife, househusband, business executive, blue-collar worker, student, or _____. This is my label.

Why am I: This is my reason for living or existing.

Our self-concept is usually built upon the way we have been answering these questions. It is our sense of being somebody. Let's go a step further and complete the section below. "I am _____" means I am this type of person and this is how I feel about myself.

I am _____

I am _____

I am _____

I am _____

Put a P by every positive statement.
Put an N by every negative statement.
Put FM if statement is true because another family member has said so.
Put F if statement is true because a friend has said so.
Put G if statement is true because God says so.
Put U if statement is true but is unconfirmed by anybody.

"In Christ" we have a godly self-image –

1. We are objects of his great love: John 3.16; Romans 5.8; Romans 8.1–4.
2. We are objects of great value to him: Galatians 2.20; 1 Corinthians 6.19–20; Ephesians 2.8–10.

OPTION THREE: FRIENDSHIPS AND THEIR EFFECTS ON YOU

Get into groups of five. Everyone should get a *Friends* sheet (see below) to fill out on another person in the room. You can make sure that each person has a sheet filled out on him or her by making sure each person's name is on a sheet before handing them out. Collect the sheets and give each person the sheet that describes them. Discuss everyone's feelings. Point out how genuine support can build up a relationship and make it strong.

Friends

Name _____

What does this person remind you of and why?

a. colour_____

b. flower _____

c. part of a car_____

d. animal _____

Why do you like this person? _____

_____

What are this person's strong points? _____

_____

Why is this person so interesting? _____

_____

GENERAL SESSION

Get everyone to complete the *Agree/Disagree* questionnaire (see next pages). Then put it on the overhead projector. Divide the room so that one side is the *Agree* side and the other is the *Disagree* side. Go down the list to point out the right answers. Occasionally stop and get everyone to go to the side of the room which matches their answer to the question. Discuss why they answered the statement the way they did. Spend 25 minutes on this part of the exercise.

Hand out the next sheet – *Sexuality* (see below) and divide the group into teams of five.

Assign to each group an area under the five headings and get them to read the scripture verses mentioned. Provide groups with concordances and chain reference or study Bibles so they can find more information on that topic. The assignment is to paraphrase in their own words the meaning of sexuality as it applies to the specific area they are working on. Ask the teams to jot down questions they or their friends have in that area.

Sexuality is defined in broad terms as, "The whole person (thoughts, experiences, ideas, values and imaginings) as he or she relates to being male or female. It is the power to relate as a person."

After the groups have finished their task, let them share their results as one big group. Recap what has been said and end in prayer.

Saturday Evening
Use Saturday evening for a talent night or talent show.

Sexuality

Emotional: 1 Corinthians 7.2–9; 1 Thessalonians 4.3–8

Intellectual: Matthew 15.19–20; Romans 12.1–2

Social: Leviticus 18.20, 22

Spiritual: Ephesians 5.25–33

Physical: Psalm 139

☐ ☐   ☐☐☐☐☐☐   ☐   ☐   ☐

Agree/Disagree

Put a tick beside each statement you agree with.

1. The two most important facts about us as human beings are:
   a. We were born with the mind and body of a human being.
   b. We are all sexual, all of our lives, each unique in our own way at any given moment.

2. Six features of human personality are:
   a. God made us rational beings – creatures sharing intelligence.
   b. God made us creatures of affect (the ability to share emotions).
   c. God made us creatures who must obey his every bidding.
   d. God made us creatures with little understanding of values.
   e. God made us with the ability to be conscious of ourselves.
   f. God gave us a temporary spirit.

3. Intercourse is a language of the body.

4. Intimate self-disclosure through sexual intercourse invites self-disclosure at all other levels of personal existence.

5. I am really one person – my body and mind are one.

☐☐   ☐   ☐   ☐☐☐ ☐ ☐ ☐ ☐   ☐ ☐

6. In God's mind, our bodies are:

    a. a temple   d. useful for his service
    b. flesh and blood   e. good
    c. corrupted

    ☐ ☐ ☐

7. Jesus was sexless.

8. "I desired all things, that I might enjoy life; God gave me life, that I might enjoy all things."

9. Sexual fantasizing:

    a. is right
    b. is useful to relieve boredom
    c. puts us in a state of false euphoria and mindlessness.

10. Every person is a rock or an island – not needing help or support.

11. People are slaves of whatever has mastered them.

12. Where your sexuality is, there will your heart be.

13. Sexuality is learnt as we socialize and interact with others.

14. The way we think and feel about ourselves as bodies will always find expression in the way we think and feel about the world and about God.

15. Human sexuality equals sex and sex equals genital sex acts.

Sunday morning

After breakfast and devotions everyone could spend several minutes writing down questions they would like to ask about the areas they dealt with on Saturday.

Then have a session with a panel of sponsors and adults answering the questions which were submitted in writing.

Follow this with a worship service, maybe using creative drama and choral reading.

Programme 3

Helping each other

The people Don't impose this design on your young people. If you think the topic and direction are useful for them, share the idea with them. Let those young people help design the weekend's goals and purposes. If they don't become involved in setting the goals, you may be wasting everyone's time. But if the design meets needs and speaks to concerns, get ready for an exciting time!

The place Weekend centres and sites vary greatly in what they offer and what they leave for you to do. This design is intended for a place where meals are prepared by staff and not by the group itself. Should your centre require time for cooking meals, setting tables, etc., adjustments to the design can be made easily both before and after meals. If your budget is very small, think of options such as visiting a church in another town or someone's house. Many weekends have flourished with sleeping bags on gym mats for accommodation.

Preparation

Weekend activities help build good group relationships. At the same time they depend on good group interaction. Give some time (at least two meetings) prior to the weekend for thought and planning with those committed to the experience.

Use or adapt the following ideas for those optional meetings.

Goal setting Share the weekend's goals and purposes with the entire group. Then pass out paper and pencils and get everyone to answer the following questions:

- What are my reasons for attending this weekend?
- What's one thing I hope to gain from it?
- What am I willing to do to make this a good experience for myself and for others in the group?

In groups of four to six, allow time for people to share their responses.

What really annoys me The first weekend session calls for role plays on the topic, "What really annoys me about other people". Divide into groups of three or four and let each group secretly practise a two-to-three-minute sketch to be presented on the weekend.

Creative devotions teams Divide volunteers into two teams. Challenge your devotion groups to use themes that deal with our helping, supporting, caring relationships. Among others, the teams might consider Luke 15.11–24; Luke 10.25–37; Galatians 6.1–2; John 13.4–9. Teams can use music, records, sketches or readings to close the day's activities. Allow plenty of time for practice. You may want to help in the planning stages.

A "typical situation" Try a fun activity that will help your group see a need for the weekend. Come up with a typical youth group activity. Then write on pieces of paper different roles to be acted out. For instance, the activity might be "deciding which group game to play". The goal is to come to a group consensus. Different roles can be "leader, wants to play volleyball", "leader, wants to play charades", "sad over lost boy/girlfriend", "angry with any leader", "doesn't like anything", "will agree to anything", and so on. After the activity has become totally frustrating, stop it and ask the different actors their feelings about themselves and the other actors.

Group covenant A covenant (a promise between two or more persons) can be a meaningful commitment made by group members to each other. Get each group member to complete and sign the covenant (see next page).

A brief meeting prior to the weekend can reaffirm the covenant and confirm details such as meeting times, departure times, equipment to bring.

Friday evening (1½ hours)
You won't have time to complete all the options in this outline. Using key young people in your planning team, plan activities

Covenant

1. We commit ourselves to treat each other as follows:

2. We will support and be responsible for each other by:

3. We expect our leaders to:

4. We agree to handle any group behaviour issues or concerns (such things as noise, sleeping times, alcohol, hassles/disagreements, and breaking the covenant) in the following way:

5. As a group on this weekend we want to accomplish: (list the group's goals)

Signatures _____

_____

_____

and studies that will best suit your group.

1. Begin with an icebreaker: *Spring Beauty Contest.* Provide stacks of old newspaper (you'll need plenty), several pairs of scissors, rolls of sticky tape and an abundance of pins.
   Divide into groups of four or five persons each and make sure each group has the necessary supplies. You'll also need a separate room or corner where each group can work secretly.
   Each group selects one person to be its entrant in the

"beauty" contest. After deciding what person, place, thing or animal the entrant is to be, everyone goes to work – cutting, crumpling, bunching, rolling, piecing, pinning, taping. Allow 15 minutes. Then call everybody together for a costume show and an awarding of small prizes.

2. *Name tags* – provide a large piece of paper, a pin and a felt tip pen for each person. The object is to tear the paper into the shape of an animal that represents you. (Use a large piece of newspaper to show, step by step, what you mean.)

On one half of the large name tag, get everyone to write two little-known facts about themselves and then a lie. On the other half of the name tag, each person follows these directions:

a. Write a brief definition of "help".
b. Jot down one reason people need help.
c. The kind of person I look for when I need help is…
d. When people come to me for help, it's usually because…

Allow enough time for everyone to complete each item.

Divide into small groups and get each person to explain what his or her "animal" is. After guessing which statements are true and which one is the lie, each person shares answers to the sentences on helping. Encourage people to explain why they wrote what they did.

3. *What really annoys me about other people* – if you prepared the sketches outlined earlier, put them on now.

4. *Forehead feelings* – stick a large label to each person's forehead. Use a marker to write a feeling on each one ("happy", "sad", "angry", "depressed", "lovesick", "lonely", "put upon", "happy-go-lucky", and so on). Get each person to try to guess what feeling he has on his forehead by the way people act towards him. For instance, people would treat the "happy" label as though he or she is happy. After the exercise, ask different people how they felt being treated the way they were.

5. Bible study: *Honesty: The first step in helping* (see next page) – the Bible study will work best when you use it as a worksheet which includes both the passage to be studied and the

Bible study: Honesty, the first step in helping

"LOGS AND SPECKS" Read Matthew 7.1–5 and then answer the following questions.

1. My first reaction to "logs and specks" is: (choose one)
   - ☐ Surprise! I never thought of my own weaknesses as "specks in the eye", not to mention "logs".
   - ☐ Concern! I'm wondering if some people see "logs" in my eyes, and I think they're just "specks".
   - ☐ So what's new? Everybody has problems.
   - ☐ Other:

2. One of my problems with "logs and specks" is (choose one)
   - ☐ I never really seem to spot any specks in others. I suppose I'm just too trusting.
   - ☐ You wouldn't believe the kinds of specks I see in others. Everyone is full of faults. It's amazing!
   - ☐ It's hard to notice that log in my own eye, even when I strongly suspect there is one there.
   - ☐ I don't look beyond the specks or logs sometimes, but just tend to judge the person on what I see at first glance.
   - ☐ Other:

3. The kind of specks I really find it easy to notice in people are: (tick any that apply)
   - ☐ People who are friendly in class but ignore you outside it.
   - ☐ People who act as if they're too good for you.
   - ☐ People who act as if they're perfect, but then really come unstuck.
   - ☐ Other:

4. To be perfectly honest, some of the logs in my life that I struggle with from time to time are: _____

   _____

5. Knowing that I have logs to deal with makes me: _____

   _____

6. One thing Jesus is saying loud and clear to me through these words from Matthew is:_____

   _____

discussion questions.

Complete the Bible study in the small groups, with each person completing the response questions after reading the text. (Allow 30 minutes for this exercise).

6. Closing devotion.

Saturday morning (2 hours)

1. *Wake up or lose your socks* – on the floor mark a circle that's large enough to seat the whole group. Everybody who sits in the circle is shoeless, but is wearing socks. On a "go" signal, the object is to collect as many socks as possible. The people who lose their socks are out of the game (and the circle). They're also out of the game if any part of their body goes outside the circle. The last person in the circle wins.

2. *Group survey* – hand out pencils and postcards, four cards to each person. Then ask the following questions (one answer for each card):

   a. One thing that makes me angry is…
   b. I really like it when people…
   c. One thing the youth group can do to make me feel more accepted is…
   d. One thing I'm struggling with right now is…

   Collect the cards. Use one large strip of paper for each question and collate the answers while the groups are working through the following Bible study. Post the survey responses for everyone to see.

3. Bible study: *What, me lost?* (see next page) – this is a good time to arrange new groups so that relationships are extended beyond just four to six people. Get the two people from each group whose birthdays are closest to the weekend date to switch groups. The rest of the group remain intact. The group reads Luke 15.1–7 together.

4. *What's that?* – a first step in helping someone is being able to understand what he or she is trying to say. To get practice in listening, try this exercise: divide into groups of three. Explain that you'll read a statement and each person will have up to three minutes to talk about it while the other two listen. The "talker" can either agree or disagree with the

statement or add new thoughts.

The "listeners" are to try to understand the speaker's feelings and beliefs. They can ask questions to clarify what the speaker is saying, but may not comment or add thoughts. They should also keep eye contact with the speaker.

After all have expressed themselves, ask the entire group to comment on how they felt and what principles of listening they learnt. Various listening topics are:

a. Boys are better than girls because…
b. Girls are better than boys because…

Bible study:

"What, me lost?"

Read Luke 15.1–7 and answer the following questions:

1. The part of this scripture that really spoke clearly to me was:

   _____

   _____

2. Some of the ways people I know seem to get lost today are:

   _____

   _____

3. I feel lost when:

   _____

   _____

4. Some people have been able to "find" me in my life and bring me back when I have been "lost". What they have usually done is:

   _____

   _____

c. God guides our lives every second.

Use some of the responses to the group survey if you think they'll make adequate discussion topics.

Saturday afternoon (2 hours)

1. *Amoeba Race* – tie a long rope around each group that formed in the last session. Set up a course for the teams to run, perhaps to one end of the room, over an obstacle and back again. Race two teams at a time until you have a winner. To guard against crunched toes, all team members should remove their shoes.
2. *Over My Head* – read Matthew 14.22–33. Assign roles and read the passage as a dramatic reading. The roles needed are: narrator, several disciples, Jesus, Peter.
3. After the dramatic reading, pass out sheets of paper and ask everyone to write the following items:

   a. One word that describes my feelings after hearing this story.
   b. The strongest truth I see coming out of this story is ...
   c. Like Peter, I sometimes get in "over my head". When I do, it usually has to do with... (Possible examples are family hassles; someone of the opposite sex; making decisions; plans for the future.)
   d. Think of people whom you know who seem to be "in over their heads". What are some ways in which you might be able to reach out to them? (Again, provide

---

Problem-solving steps

Step 1. Identify and clarify all aspects of the problem.

Step 2. Try to identify what led to the problem.

Step 3. Once you've identified the problem and its causes, look at its consequences.

Step 4. What are potential solutions?

Step 5. What's the best solution, based on the information you have?

---

adequate time for sharing, encouraging each group to close with prayer).

4. *On the Spot* – this exercise is a story or situation that forces you to make a choice. It also gives everyone practice working through an important problem-solving process.

   Talk through the problem-solving steps opposite before working through any "on the spot" situations, or the ones below.

Saturday evening (2½ hours)

1. *Teeth Teasing* – the entire group sits in a circle. The object is never to show your teeth. To speak, you pull your lips inwards around your teeth to hide them.

   One person starts by asking the person next to him, "Is Mrs Mumble home?" The person responds, "I don't know; I'll have to ask my neighbour." This keeps going around the circle. When someone's teeth show, he's out. Smiling is permitted provided the teeth don't show. When asking or

---

"On the spot" situations

Situation 1. A new person is going to your school. She seems as though she'd make a good friend. But as you get to know this person you realize that her outgoing personality was a big front, that she's got the worst inferiority complex in the world. Today she stops you and says,
"There's just no hope for me. I'm stuck with being me and I hate it." How would you respond?

Situation 2. There is a film you've been wanting to see for some time but couldn't find anyone to go with. Finally you decide to go alone because the film is playing its last day. You're about to leave when the doorbell rings. There stands John, your best friend. He looks really upset. "I've got to talk to you now," he says in a whisper. "Things are bad at home. I don't know what to do." Just then the phone rings – it's another friend, Tom. "Hey, all right, you talked me into it! I'll pick you up in 15 minutes and we'll see that show!" What would you do?

Optional topics. Take various responses from the group survey question, "One thing I'm struggling with right now is…"

answering, contorting the facial muscles is okay to make the person next to you laugh.

The last one left is the winner.

2. *Conflict Is* – it's time to change two more members in each group. Get the youngest and oldest member of each group to change groups. Then allow 15 minutes for each group to come up with a brief role play that illustrates a conflict people often face.

   After the role plays, list different conflicts that group members have faced. Also refer to the group survey question, "One thing that really makes me angry is..."

3. Bible Study: *Don't Just Stand There* (see below) – hand out copies of the Bible study. When everyone has finished, begin the sharing in small groups.

4. *Conflict time* – discuss various ways of handling conflict when it arises in the group. (Some examples: denying that the problem exists, avoiding the problem, giving in to the other person, overpowering the other person, working through the problem.) List the different responses on paper.

Bible study: "Don't just stand there!"

Read 1 John 3.11–18 and tick the reactions you agree with.

1. Reading this text makes me feel:

   ☐ Challenged to help as much as I possibly can.
   ☐ Guilty! I don't really seem to be able to help a great deal.
   ☐ Frustrated. I can only do so much!
   ☐ Good. It is possible to help people from time to time.
   ☐ Other: _____

2. The message that comes through the strongest to me is:

   ☐ Helping people means actions, not just nice words.
   ☐ It is easier to "talk" help than "do" it.
   ☐ Helping people by actions is one way of showing your love for God.
   ☐ Our words about love for God have little meaning without actions of love towards people.
   ☐ Other: _____

Next, hand out sheets of paper and pencils and ask everyone to list three conflicts they have now or can remember
having. Then get each person to list what they think is their
personal style of handling the conflict and what they'd like
their personal style to be.
Take a couple of conflicts from volunteers and get the small
groups to determine alternative ways of handling the conflicts.

5. Closing devotions.

Sunday morning (2 hours)
Choose one of the two sessions, depending on the needs and
interests of your group.

OPTION 1: CREATE YOUR OWN WORSHIP SERVICE
A particularly meaningful worship experience can be created by
dividing the group up into work groups to devise an instant
worship service. Here are some possible areas to work on:

1. the worship setting – work on design, decorations, etc.;
2. music;
3. a message or sermon from the Bible;
4. a celebration of the Lord's Supper – if this is appropriate for
    your group – or prayers.

Provide appropriate materials, particularly for the music and
message teams. Let all the groups know they have two hours in
which to pull the worship service together and prepare it. You'll
find it a rewarding experience if you've never done it before.

OPTION 2: HELPING, ONE MORE TIME
Meet once more in your small groups. Volunteers in each group
read the texts used in the four previous Bible studies: Matthew
7.1–5; Luke 15.1–7; Matthew 14.22–33, and 1 John 3.11–18.
After all the four sections of scripture are ready, hand out
sheets of paper and share the following comments for individual response:

1. The section of scripture that had the most impact on me
    was...
    The reason it had the impact was...

2. One thing I learnt about helping people was...
3. One thing I discovered about being helped was...
4. One thing that surprised me in these Bible studies was...

Allow time for everyone to finish writing responses. Then move into small groups of four to six for this last sharing. Allow ample time as the ability to share will have grown over the number of studies used. Again, ask each group to close with prayer. You might consider chain prayers, each person contributing, if your group is comfortable with that.

EVALUATION:

Provide a brief evaluation form which includes questions similar to the following:

1. The best part of the weekend has been...
2. The part I liked least about the weekend was...
3. If we did another one next week I would change...
4. One thing I'll never forget about this weekend was...

Allow people time to finish writing. Assure them that they need not put their names on their evaluation sheets. Read them carefully in reviewing the weekend.

Programme 4

Parents and teenagers

The psychology of adolescence

What looks like downright rebellion from teenagers is probably a normal task an adolescent performs in the process of becoming an adult. Keith Olson, a Christian clinical psychologist, said youth leaders need to understand adolescent behaviour in order to minister to their group and individuals.

"WHO AM I?"

Olson said the adolescent's primary psychological task is the search for self-identity, which has at least five characteristics.

1. Self-ideal: how a young person sees him- or herself in the future. Long- and short-range goals are set. Some wish they could be like a certain person. Others aim for a mixture of values: honest, courageous, strong-willed, hard-working, generous, and so on.

2. Self-concept: how a young person perceives him- or herself. Self-concept changes each day.

3. Self-evaluation: how the adolescent compares self-ideal and self-concept. The greater the distance between the two, the harder the struggle for self-identity.

4. Self-valuation: even if the adolescent has a fairly accurate self-concept and realistic goals, they may not see the value of their life. Part of self-identity is a sense of being created by God and having a purpose in God's world.

5. Self as the focus of power: adolescents become less and less dependent upon others as they leave childhood.

COMMON ADOLESCENT BEHAVIOURS

As adolescents search for the answer to "who am I?" several common behaviours tend to manifest themselves. Olson outlined four of these.

1. Preoccupation with body. Most adolescents do not like their bodies. There is a fear of how one's rapidly changing frame will finally look in adulthood. A few with well-proportioned bodies tend to focus most of their identity on it, all the time fearing others will discover little of value underneath the skin.

2. Development of social relationships. As adolescents break away from their families, they begin a surrogate family among peers. The pressures of peer groups are normal and intense as adolescents work at building friendships.

3. Dramatic reactions. Adolescents feel roller-coaster emotions. As they discover more and more of themselves, however, emotions tend to stabilize.

4. Dependence versus independence. Usually called rebellion, this is the struggle between dependence on parents and the development of independence. The adolescent constantly faces confusion whether to act as a child or as an adult. For example, a girl, 15, accepts a date with a man, 22. Her parents do not allow her to keep the date. She resents their "attack" on her independence and complains to her friends how rotten her parents are. Yet the dependent child within her is relieved that her parents saved her from a date she feared and didn't want to keep anyway. As the adolescent finds out more of his or her identity, responsible independent behaviour will eventually evolve, an adult living without depending on parents.

Planning committee meeting

Gather together three from the youth group, two parents, one youth leader and overall youth coordinator or minister.

1. Set goals for the weekend, for example:

    a. To help young people and parents understand each other's roles and concerns.
    b. To understand the challenges of adolescence.
    c. To help young people and parents communicate, share and listen.

d. To allow young people to share with one another and parents with other parents.

2. Outline plan for weekend.
3. Decide responsibilities, select menu, and secure resources.
4. Set rules for the weekend – they should be agreed upon through discussion by planning committee.
5. Who will go? How will they be invited?

This weekend is for both young people and parents. Be certain to allow adequate time for the young people to share among themselves, and likewise the parents.

Friday evening

1. All Together Now – use the resource list at the end of the

---

A prayer to be used during the weekend

Lord, who am I?

Sometimes I really don't know. And other times I really know me – who I am, where I am going, what I want to do with my life.

Sometimes I really like myself – other times I can't stand to be with me. Why? What is it that makes me one way one moment – and another way the next moment?

Sometimes I really am confused about what I believe, other times I really know what it is I believe. Sometimes I feel so hassled, I just want to get away from people, but some of the time I can hardly wait to see my friends, to be with my family.

Lord, who am I?

Help me to know me. Help me to be able to touch that inside me which is most me. Help me to sort through all my doubts, fears, and hopes; till I discover who I really am and how I fit into my family. How I fit into your plans.

Thank you, Lord, for just listening. Thank you, Lord, for caring about me. I know you love me – and you are with me as I discover myself more fully.

Amen.

book for group game ideas.
2. Family Picture – hand out sheets of paper and crayons and ask people to draw pictures of their families. Divide into groups of three or four and ask each person to explain his or her drawing to the group.
3. Speaker and Discussion Groups – enlist the help of a qualified speaker to speak on the topic, *What Does It Mean To Be a Family?*
After the talk, divide into groups of six parents and six young people in each group. (Divide your group accordingly if you end up with an odd number of either group.) Begin by putting the parents in a circle with the young people sitting in another circle outside the parents. The parents do all the talking; the young people must remain silent and listen. After 10-15 minutes or so, switch and put the young ones in the inner circle. They do all the talking while the parents listen.
4. Closing celebration – singing, telling stories, conducting a Bible study and using the prayer on the previous page are a few ideas for this time period.
5. Get each person to complete the family survey (see pages 110 – 111).

Saturday morning

1. Games and singing – be sure to choose activities and songs both parents and teenagers will enjoy.
2. Speaker and discussion groups – find a dynamic person who's qualified to speak on the topic, *Getting Along With Myself.* Use *The Psychology of Adolescence*, page 105, as the basis for discussion.
3. Personal reflection time – allow 15 minutes for everyone to find a quiet place and reflect on "Who am I?" and "How can I really be 'me' in my family?"

Saturday afternoon

1. Crazy exercises – get a parent or teenager to lead everyone in a few funny exercises. Aerobic exercises are usually fun to try in a large group. Or have a laugh working out to one of

the exercise records on the market.

2. Discussion – plan a small group discussion period. Encourage the parents and young people to meet in the same groups for this activity, and discuss the relationships between parents and teenagers – the joys and difficulties!

3. Panel discussion – beforehand, ask three young people and three adults to meet for a panel discussion. Questions you might want to ask:

- How can you make things easier for your parents/teenagers to talk with you?
- How can parents and teenagers learn to listen?
- What things need to happen for parents and young people to trust one another better?
- What are creative ways to settle arguments?

Hand out slips of paper and pencils. Ask everyone to jot down questions they'd like to ask the panel and give the papers to you. Check the questions; put them to the panel for answering.

4. Free time – plan structured activities, encourage parents and the youth group to spend this time together.

Saturday evening

1. Family games – consult the resource list at the end of the book for ideas on games and activities families can take part in together.

2. Divide into teams of three with adults and young people on the same teams. Give each team one of the following situations to role play:

- Sibling rivalry
- Coming in too late
- Wanting the car
- Use of drugs
- Wanting more freedom

Each team is to plan its role play with two outcomes: conflict resolved, and conflict unresolved. Allow 10–15 minutes for the teams to plan their role plays. Then get each team to show its two role plays to the entire group.

Family survey

Directions. Tick the response which best expresses your feelings. Where appropriate, write your own brief response.

1. Of all the crisis situations which could (and do) occur in your family, the one you would have (have had) the most difficulty handling is:

☐ Death of a family member ☐ Divorce
☐ Serious illness ☐ Alcoholism or drug abuse in family
☐ Destruction of home by flood, storm, fire.

2. You have just received a phone call from your minister who informed you that your teenage daughter is at his house and is in trouble. All the way over to his house you try to anticipate what the trouble might be. Upon your arrival your minister informs you that he has bailed your daughter out of jail after she had been arrested for public drunkenness. Your immediate response is: Thank God it (she) wasn't (isn't):

☐ Worse ☐ Injured ☐ Pregnant ☐ On drugs ☐ Running away

3. How do you express the Christian faith with each other in your family? _____

4. The television programme your are watching is suddenly interrupted with the startling news that enemy nuclear bombs will be falling throughout the country within 30 minutes. With less then 30 minutes to live, you reflect on your past life and you decide the chief regret you have is:

☐ Not seeing my children grow up
☐ That I did not accomplish what I wanted
☐ That I did not help others enough
☐ That I did not show enough love
☐ That I did not share Christ with enough people

5. Your teenager's steady date for the last six months has just terminated the relationship. Your teenager is really "down". What do you say in order to help him/her feel better?
   - ☐ Want to talk?
   - ☐ I love you.
   - ☐ It really hurts, doesn't it?
   - ☐ Time will heal
   - ☐ Nothing

6. There are many forms of abuse which humans inflict on each other including various forms of physical, psychological, and spiritual abuse. Some forms are more serious than others, but we are all guilty of at least occasionally abusing those whom we love most. The most common way parents abuse children is:
   - ☐ Smacking
   - ☐ Critical attitude
   - ☐ Losing temper
   - ☐ Not listening
   - ☐ Ignoring them
   - ☐ Neglect

7. The most common way children abuse parents is:
   - ☐ Playing one against the other
   - ☐ Disregarding parent's values
   - ☐ Disobedience
   - ☐ Fighting with sibling(s)
   - ☐ Not talking with them
   - ☐ Running away

8. Parents often unjustly mistrust their teenagers. The primary reason for this is:
   - ☐ They were once teenagers too
   - ☐ Overprotectiveness
   - ☐ Lack of confidence as parents
   - ☐ Previous track record
   - ☐ Lack of communication

9. Describe your family in three sentences or less. _____

10. I get along best with my family when (describe the event or time): _____
_____
_____

3. Parental authority – explore the use of parental authority by dividing into small groups and asking each person to complete the following open-ended sentences:

    - I enjoy my parents when...
    - I think that I am mature enough for my parents to...
    - The most serious disagreement with my parents was...
    - I wish they would understand that I am...

4. Bible discussion – Read Ephesians 6.1–4 and answer the following questions:

    - Why does the Bible hold parents responsible for providing guidance?
    - Why are parents warned not to provoke anger in children?
    - What decisions should be made jointly between parents and young people?
    - What decisions should young people be allowed to make on their own?

5. List of Rights – divide into two teams of six to eight parents and young people in each group. The objective is to come up with a Bill of Rights for Youth and Parents.

A List of Rights might look something like this:

1. The right to be heard
2. The right to participate in family and individual decisions
3. The right to be loved and to love
4. The right to be yourself
5. The right to food and shelter
6. The right to safety
7. The right to be honest
8. The right to make a mistake
9. The right to your own things
10. The right to privacy

Ask representatives of each team to read their team's List of Rights to the entire group. Then choose the top ten items to make a "super" version of the List of Rights.

Sunday morning

Use whatever you like from the following worship session to create your own memorable weekend service.

CELEBRATE: FRIENDSHIPS AND FAMILY

Reflect. We are a Christian community. We are concerned for each other. We care. In this time and place we say to each other that we are here as friends in Christ. In a touch, in a smile, a handshake, a song, or common bond, we will care for each other and be cared for by each other.

Say together:

We gather to celebrate –
to worship the living God.
We gather to get closer to each other's human life,
to encounter God,
to share our love with God and friends,
to get in touch with who we are and where we are going,
to live more fully like Christ Jesus,
to grow in faith, hope and joy
and to be alive and new.

Singing: Choose a song which celebrates our relationship with God.

Listening: Read Ephesians 4.1–6.

If we are to grow more like Christ, then we need to take a closer look at ourselves.

Confession:

Lord,
We're uptight about so much these days,
    we wash our hands, our faces, our lives because we want to
        be clean.
But we're still uptight
    and we want to be free. Free to live and love and rejoice!
So, Lord,
    make life holy,
purify the obscenities that disturb us. Open us up to each other;
    intensify relationships; create conversations.

Help men and women talk more to one another,
  do more, cry and laugh more, care more together.
Help the young live out their full life
  with their senses open, that they may enter adult life fulfilled,
    freed.
Help adults complete their lives
  with purpose in what they do, freed of the weight of frustra-
    tion.
Let us each be what we are intended to be;
  a part of your world, a part of your family, a lover and friend,
and let us seek the mystery in each other.
Give us awe and wonder.
Give us the freedom of the Christ
  who loves us all as brother and sister and who does every-
    thing we allow him to do to make us holy and glad. Amen.

Silent reflection and meditation.

A new community: Thomas Merton writes:

Certain ones, very few are our close friends. Because we have more in common with them, we are able to love them with a special selfless perfection, since we have more to share. They are inseparable from our own destiny, and therefore, our love for them is especially holy.

Share with two or three others what Merton's words mean for you.

Now share with one other person the meaning of these words.

Passing the peace:

In the church's earliest manifestations, there was a keen appreciation of touch. Touch was the encounter through which love, commissioning, forgiveness, punishment, and communion were conveyed. Christ and his followers were sensitive to man's need for an incarnational dimension to the Word of God. The fact of God being fleshed out in Jesus Christ was not just something to be seen. Christ came not to give words about God. Through him the people could "press the flesh" and know that God is good.

                                          Dennis Benson

Pass the peace among one another.

A deeper look at community (relationships)
Read Galatians 5.13–15, 22–25

Reflection

Community is more than contact; it is caring, compassion, concern, comforting, creating, celebrating, conversing, communion and service. Community is always becoming – never complete. Two or more share life together, risking to show pain, loneliness, fears, angers; receiving understanding, support, encouragement, and relationship. Community involves risking error for another's sake, losing oneself for a great cause, responding to a need for enhancing the qualitative character of human life. Thank God for community in the making.

W Stanley Smith Jr

Singing: Choose a song that emphasizes Christian fellowship.

A CLOSER LOOK AT FRIENDSHIP AND RELATIONSHIP

Prayer
O Lord, I need to learn – I need you to teach me how to handle my relationships with people. Teach me the difference between being sensitive to the needs and desires of others, and the game we sometimes play with each other; between speaking the truth in love and meddling where I do not belong; between being bold, brave and strong, and being pushy and bossy.

Help me to understand and practise the meaning of love – and remind me that it sometimes means gently admonishing someone else I care about, and at other times it means keeping my mouth shut.

Show me how to be flexible and adapt to the needs and circumstances of each person I meet and know. Help me to bend, to change, to listen, but not to go beyond my own beliefs and convictions.

I need to learn how to touch and not to grab, to encourage, but not to put down and judge, to love and care but also to remember that my loving and caring touches many lives, and some need me more than others. Help me to make good use of my time, so that the deep commitments really get my energy and time. Give me the sensitivity to know when someone needs to be alone, and when someone needs a friend.

Singing: Choose a song which reminds us of the need to become more like Jesus in our community and relationships.

WE ARE MEMBERS OF CHRIST'S COMMUNITY

Reading: Romans 12.1–5. Describe in your own words the meaning of community.

LITANY FOR NEW POSSIBILITY

LEADER: Let us pray for the virtues we would like to possess, the virtues that will bring new possibilities for human existence. Let us not be listless or unconcerned, never taking positions or getting involved with the world and the people around us.

COMMUNITY: God, we would be alive – alive to the people around us, alive to our families, alive to the world and its concerns, alive to our own thoughts and feelings. God, we pray for life.

LEADER: Let us not be frightened, anxious about everything we say or do, fearful that it may not be the "right" thing.

COMMUNITY: Lord, we would be confident – confident in the truth you have revealed to us; confident in the love you have shown for us; confident in the new kinds of relationships you have granted to us. Lord, we pray for confidence.

LEADER: But let us not be overbearing in our positions, never accepting the possibility that we might be wrong, always insisting that others must see and do things our way.

COMMUNITY: God, we would be open – open to new ideas, new insights, open to each other, open to suggestions from parent or spouse. God, we pray for a spirit of openness.

LEADER: Let us not give up before the end, turning away when things go wrong, dropping

commitments before they have been brought
to fulfilment in God's good time.

COMMUNITY: Lord, we would be courageous – steadfast in
our faith, dedicated to our commitment,
strong in carrying out the promises we have
made to live as your Son's disciples. Lord, we
would be faithful.
Amen.

Singing: Finish with a strong song of praise and fellowship.

Programme 5

Blessed are the peacemakers

This weekend has several options to help your group to explore peacemaking both on the personal and the international level. The group will delve more deeply into the biblical concepts of Shalom than most have before. They will discover that Scripture questions some assumptions they may have about violence, communication and patriotism. This should be a time for fun, but also an occasion for learning new skills for handling conflict and studying the issues of war and peace.

Before the weekend

1. Carefully read the outline, meet with other leaders and interested young people and choose from the options.
2. Round up the recommended supplies and equipment.

   Supplies: plenty of Bibles, Bible study aids, recommended books and pamphlets, paper, pencils, biographies of peacemakers, such as Francis of Assisi, William Penn, Martin Luther King Jr, Gandhi, etc.
   Equipment: slide projector/video recorder, record and tape player.

3. Order any audio-visuals to be used. When they arrive preview them and make arrangements for someone to show them.
4. Duplicate any questions, quotes, rules or worship sheets the group will need.

Friday evening

Arrive, unpack and settle in. After supper gather together. This is a good time for group singing or warm-up games. Welcome everyone, go over the housekeeping rules, introduce the plan of the weekend and general topic.

SESSION 1: CONFLICTS IN OUR WORLD

OPTION 1 INTRODUCTION

Put this question to the group:

"As long as there are two humans, there will be conflicts. The problem is not just the conflict, but how to resolve it. Both are important. What are some conflicts in your own life, at home and school, locally, nationally and internationally?"

(Either pass out paper for each member to write his or her own list or get the group to call out suggestions as you write them on a flip chart or large sheet of paper.)

A few conflicts the group might list:

Between parents and children: cleaning room, doing chores, what to wear, what to watch on TV, when to come home, choice of friends.

Between parents: how money is spent, where to live, friends, how to discipline children.

Between brothers and sisters: use of toys/possessions, use of bathroom, chores, what to watch on TV.

At school: homework, results, classroom discipline, personality of teacher, dress rules, morals and values of peers.

In the community: law and order, tax assessments, etc.

Nationally: industrial relations, racial issues, environmentalists and chemical companies, peacemakers and Ministry of Defence and arms manufacturers.

Internationally: Russia versus United States, Israel versus Arabs, Irish Catholics versus Irish Protestants, Sikhs versus Hindus in India, Pakistan versus India over Kashmir, China versus Russia, China versus Taiwan, dictators versus guerrillas, North versus South Korea, rich versus poor in many Latin American countries, whites versus blacks in South Africa and neighbouring states.

How can the above conflicts be resolved (or how are they being resolved)?

Locally and personally: by shouting and arguing, divorce and separation, talking and reasoning things out, ignoring the problem, agreeing to disagree, "cold war".

Nationally: by debates, letters to editors and MPs, influencing and passing legislation, supporting candidates for political office, strikes and boycotts, joining movements and special groups, terrorism.

Internationally: by propaganda, raising the issue at the UN through diplomatic channels, special envoys and negotiators, building up arms, terrorism, breaking off diplomatic relations, embargoes and boycotts, secret attempts to undermine a nation's economy, conventional war, nuclear war.

OPTION 2 INTRODUCTION

Have on hand stacks of old newspapers. Divide the group into smaller groups of four or five. Let each person select a newspaper or magazine, read a story about conflict, and share it with members of the small groups. (Choosing and reading should take about 5–8 minutes, sharing it with each other about 8–10 minutes.)

After a suitable time, call the groups together and ask them to share the types of conflicts they discovered. List these on a blackboard or flip chart.

After everyone has had a chance to report, go back over the list and ask how the conflicts are being resolved (or if they are). Write the methods down also: war, terrorism, negotiation, passing a new law, etc.

THE REST OF THE EVENING

1. You could show a film or slide-tape presentation on various aspects of conflict.
2. Break for recreation and refreshments.
3. A Late Show video could also be offered. While this should be of an entertainment nature, the subject of the film should relate to your theme. (I've seen too many weekends where the leaders just picked any old film to "keep the group busy".) Consider the make-up of your group as you look through the film catalogues.

Saturday morning

If you have a morning devotion, give the group several of the passages relating to peace from Matthew 5. Ask them to be thinking, "How do I measure up?"

After breakfast and cleaning up the group gets together again. The morning could be divided into two segments with a break in between.

SESSION 2: THE BIBLE AND PEACEMAKING

Have on hand Bibles, paper and pencils, and Bible study aids such as atlases, commentaries and dictionaries. Ask the members to get into the small groups they formed the night before. Tell them that they are going to study and discuss a Bible passage in depth. Point to and explain the various Bible study aids laid out on a table and the rules for sharing them, returning them, and so on. Also mention the adult leaders who will offer help. The groups are to find answers for the following: What does the passage mean for the writer's day? For the Church later on? For me today?

Give each group one or more of the following passages:

- Isaiah 2.1–4 and Micah 4.1–4;
- Isaiah 11.1–9;
- Isaiah 65.17–25;
- Ezekiel 34.17–31;
- Matthew 5.1–6; 5.21–26; 5.38–48; 7.24–27.

Give the group at least 30 minutes to study and discuss their passages. Then call them back together to share their findings.

SESSION 3: CHRIST AND CONFLICT

We've seen what Christ taught about relating to enemies in his Sermon on the Mount. For him this was no ivory tower theory or nice set of ethics to follow only if the other person would play the game too. It grew out of a deep understanding of God's Word and will for his life and ministry. We see this at the beginning of his ministry.

Ask someone to read Matthew 4.1–11. (This could be more interesting if three persons read it: one, the narrative; two, the words of the Devil; three, the dialogue of Christ.)

Ask the group: What does it mean to "be tempted by" the Devil in the context of this passage? What were the Jews longing for? How would many of them achieve their dream?

Divide into the same small groups again and let each choose one of the following passages that shed more light on Jesus' teaching about relationships and love:

1. Isaiah 53. This was part of Jesus' Bible. What style of leadership does it teach? Is there any similarity with Jesus? With the kind of lifestyle he commended to his followers? Compare that with the John Wayne or James Bond type of hero.
2. Matthew 8.5–13: Jesus and the centurion. How did most Jews feel towards the Romans? Does this seem to bother Jesus?
3. Matthew 9.9–13 and Luke 19.1–10. How were tax collectors regarded? Why? What does Jesus do about them?
4. John 4.4–9 and Luke 10.30–37. What was the relationship between Jews and Samaritans? Did Jesus go along with this? What did he do about it?
5. Luke 19.41–44 and Matthew 26.49–52. What is the result of violence? How is this borne out in history? In Northern Ireland and Palestine today?
6. Luke 23.33–47. How does Jesus react to his tormentors? What effect does this have on the thieves? On the Roman soldier? How would you feel if you had helped drive the nails into Jesus' flesh?
7. Acts 7.54—8.1. How does Stephen follow in the Lord's footsteps? What effect do you think this may have had on Saul? Could it have played a part in Saul's later conversion?

After 15–20 minutes, call the groups back together and let them report their findings. Overall, how does Christ handle conflict and hostility?

Conclude with a reading of Ephesians 2.11–18.

Saturday afternoon

RECREATION OR OPTION FOR EXTRA SESSION

Give out materials on peacemakers and share reports on them.

Ask groups to write a litany or other type of prayer on peace-making.

Saturday evening

SESSION 4: THE PSYCHOLOGY AND ETHICS OF NON-VIOLENCE
Read Romans 12.9–21. What do you think of the admonition "never take revenge"? What happens between warring groups and nations when they ignore this? How would Paul's statement in verse 20 be startling to an enemy? Read this in several translations.

The enemy expects you to react to him in the same way he treats you. When you refuse to do so, but return love for hostility, he is thrown off balance, confused. You've broken the agreement that the best way to settle differences is by violence. When the victim turns the other cheek and continues to reason with the opponent and to appeal to his better nature, he may get the other cheek slapped, and slapped again. The vicious circle of vengeance is broken, and the possibility of reconciliation exists as long as one person refuses to join in the self-perpetuating circle of hostility. As Gandhi put it, "The hardest heart and the grossest ignorance must disappear before the rising sun of suffering without anger and without malice."

Share the *Ten Commandments of Fighting Fairly* (see next page) with the group by showing them on flipchart or overhead projector. Encourage discussion.

SESSION 5: PREPARATION FOR WORSHIP
Announce to the group that the following day's worship service will include projects that they have created. Some possibilities: a peace banner, a litany or prayer(s) on peacemaking, a box collage on peace and war, sketches or role plays on peacemaking, a choral presentation of a song, meditations on any of the peace scriptures.

Here are some suggestions for projects:

Peace banners. This can be one large banner using symbols and words of love and peace. Bring along books and materials on symbols and banner making. Some groups have let individuals create small banners and then incorporated them into a large banner.

Writing litanies and prayers. Have on hand your church's worship/prayer book and other such materials to serve as models. Let volunteers look over materials (including biblical passages) and go to work.

Collages. Have boxes, old magazines, paste, poster paint/markers for volunteers to decorate. Paint large outlined peace symbols or words and fill them in with pictures. Stack the boxes up for a peace wall or into the shape of a cross. (Use a

---

The ten commandments of fighting fairly (and non-violently)

1. Remember that you and your opponent are both human, and thus fallible. Either, or both, of you might be wrong, and you thus should be open to new facts.
2. Gather your facts and state the reasons for your position as clearly as possible. Be grateful if your opponent leads you into a greater awareness of truth.
3. Never seek to humiliate your opponent. You are looking for truth, not victory. Thus, do not attack your opponent, but only facts or faulty argument.
4. Never dehumanize your opponent with labels and hostile names.
5. Beware of any note of superiority or patronizing air in your voice or body language as you present your case. The manner in which you face your opponent might be more important than your words and facts.
6. Look for the good in your opponent and his or her position. Try to find ways of appealing to the best in him or her, as well as in any onlookers. (Often sympathetic onlookers can, just by their presence, sway an opponent.)
7. Absorb the hostility of your opponent in as cheerful a manner as possible. Never return insult for insult or blow for blow.
8. Use humour when possible, but it must be directed against yourself or the situation, not your opponent.
9. Keep praying for love, patience and courage. Use the prayer of St Francis frequently in your devotions.
10. Practise the above in the little, everyday conflicts, and you will be ready if and when a major conflict arises. Keep in mind Matthew 5.10–11.

board to hold the boxes that form the arms.) Make one side to symbolize our warfare, the other Christ's peace.

Sketches. Think of situations of strife, big or small, real or fictional, and create ways that a Christian might resolve them.

Music. Bring multiple copies of folk hymnals with such songs as "Prayer of St. Francis". Encourage the group to bring guitars and other instruments.

Meditations. Bring copies of devotional materials for inspiration. You need not wait until Saturday night to begin these workshops. They could be described on Friday and the group encouraged to start work during Saturday afternoon.

Sunday morning

SESSION 6: PEACEMAKERS YOU SHOULD KNOW

Present reports, prepared by you or other youth leaders, on such peacemakers as Francis of Assisi, Mahatma Gandhi, Martin Luther King Jr, Daniel Berrigan.

Prepare for worship. Finish up or rehearse projects. Close with a creative worship service on "Shalom".

Programme 6

Experiencing blindness

All right now, people, shut those beady little eyes of yours and imagine staying like that for eighteen hours. Let me tell you, it's a real experience and I recommend anyone to try it.

We used bandages with surgical adhesive tape for the blind-folds. They are not so easily removed, and the temptation to peep is lessened. We did have a rule that blindfolds could be removed if a situation became unbearable, but in fact the need never arose.

Before the blindfolds went on, we all agreed to a contract, which essentially is a statement of the ground rules of the week-end. Then one by one, each of us lost all touch with our most indispensable sense – sight. It was the last daylight we would see until Saturday afternoon. Some of us were pretty bold in the beginning, until we learnt that one wrong move could land somebody in hospital.

"I felt awkward, clumsy and terribly dependent." One person's reaction sums up what a good many of us in the group felt.

Next on the agenda was getting from our church to the venue. This was an experience in itself. The members were completely dependent on the driver and one another's voices.

The accommodation was ideal for this weekend: an area restricted to one room with the kitchen area on the left, tables in the middle and an open area on the right. A fireplace was in the front wall with bathrooms on the opposite wall. The ceiling was high and above the bathrooms was a balcony for sleeping; it overlooked the rest of the room. Leading up to the balcony was a spiral staircase. This structure limited the extent to which people could opt out of any sessions, although in the blind portion of the weekend it would have been next to impossible anyway. Everything happened within a fairly limited area, so it simplified movement.

Getting acclimatized

For a good number of people it was the first time they had been to that venue. They were living in a place they had never seen, which I suppose isn't really that awful, since blind people never see their surroundings either.

After settling in, we did some awakening exercises that involved doing some crazy things. At first I was a little reluctant to do them for fear of the others watching me. But then I realized that everyone was in the same position, except for the helpers. Anyway, we were paired off with another person and we then had a discussion with our partner.

After that there was a short break in the schedule. Wow! That's free time! Big deal! We sat and sat and maybe once in a while someone actually spoke! It was really strange; you didn't know when to talk or really what to do or say. You were never sure if anyone was listening. Free time never went so slowly.

Then came the pizza. That you should try! It's hot; it's greasy; it's slimy; and when you can't see, it's a mess! You're never sure if you're getting it in your mouth or on your lap. Since you usually don't say much when you're eating, it's like eating alone.

Did you ever have an affair with an orange? We did! We felt it, caressed it, moved it between our hands and rolled it on our faces. Then we peeled it, eating some and squeezing the rest all over our hands until they were good and sticky. In this experience we used all our senses but sight.

Clean is a sensation you really don't fully appreciate until you're blind. We washed each other's hands with soap, water and salt, dried them and rubbed baby oil on them. After that treatment my hands actually tingled.

The last thing for the night was to experience a cup of water. Each of us was handed an empty cup and we were to realize its condition: empty, light and round. Our cup was then slowly filled with water. Listen... feel the weight change, and slowly drink it, being aware of it moving down your body.

Easier said than done

Bedtime! That's easier said than done.

First we had to describe each sleeping bag and set of belongings to find out what belonged to whom. It never occurred to us to put identification on personal belongings. Once we got the gear to the person and the person up the spiral stairs to a bed, we thought we had it made. Oh dear! Judy *had* to go down and brush her teeth. Debbie *had* to go down and wash her face. And numerous other nightly chores in the bathroom had to be done by almost everybody else... use your imagination.

Now, waking up blind is really a hairy experience when you don't know what's happening. But we all managed to work out what was going on quickly. Judy and Debbie said what they felt: "As we undid our sleeping bags to prepare for bed, I had a feeling of fear to think that when I woke up in the morning it would still be dark for me."

Come 8 a.m.! It was time for a good hearty breakfast. Most of us were moaning about how the bandages itched. And they itched as long as we sat and thought about how much they itched.

After breakfast we went on one of the most "eye-opening" (ha!) experiences of the weekend: a blind walk in the forest. We broke off into groups, one leader for every five "blindees". All six of us held hands and started out on our trip. While walking along I had a compelling fear that I was going to walk into a tree.

We then began to explore nature's wonders. Jean, our group leader, found different things and let each one of us try to work out what they were. For instance, a mint leaf. We smelled, tasted, and felt it. And because of its distinctive flavour and smell, it wasn't too hard to identify.

Judy had a good point: "Noises seemed a lot louder. Driving up in the car, the traffic and rain seemed louder. I heard things that I never took time to hear before." We walked for about half an hour. In that half hour we became unbelievably closer to nature.

One of the final blind experiences was foot washing. We each went with a partner and washed one another's feet while a story about a similar situation with Jesus and his disciples was read to us.

Vision restored

Now is the time for all good people to get rid of the blindfolds. Debbie and I sat face-to-face and slowly removed each other's blindfolds, keeping our eyes closed. And it hurt! We then counted three and opened our eyes for the first time in 18 hours, together. I imagined everything to be dull and dark. But, because of three large skylights, the room was brighter. My initial sight was a flash of light that lasted for a fraction of a second. Then I saw Debbie, and for some unknown reason, I almost started to cry.

After our sight was restored, relationships and friendships seemed much more genuine and real. Here is a statement by Roger that might help you better understand what feelings came out of the weekend: "It's hard to say what made the experience such a high point for me as well as the other participants. I can only say that when we cut off the dependence on vision, the group members became quieter and less willing to do their own thing. They gradually began to support each other so that they could walk without falling. They centred their discussion on their feelings and 'observations' and almost no time on trying to impress each other with their physical, social, or intellectual abilities. In essence, the group freed itself from the bondage of 'what will others think of me?'"

Now it's time for us to do some mind finding, soul searching or whatever you want to call it. One thing we got into was the "love process", which is basically a good set of guidelines to follow when dealing with people. The five basic steps are: I see you, I hear you, I accept your right to be you, I need you and I love you. I'll end my explanation of it there because an entire chapter could be written on it.

We also did a values clarification, which means deciding in your own head what ideas or values are most important in your life and which ideas have the least importance for you.

On Sunday, after breakfast, we had a celebration. To start, some sections of a number-one bestseller were read. Then we did *Live–Die* sheets. This is how it works: each of us took a sheet of paper and wrote on it our name and two columns – *Live* and *Die*. We all put them anywhere on the wall and began. Taking a felt-tip pen, we went to each sheet and in the *Live* column wrote a good characteristic about that person that he should let live. In the *Die* column we wrote a bad point about the individual that we thought the person should consider doing something about. At the end we all took our own sheets and read them, and if inclined to do so, discussed them with other people. I find this an excellent way of learning about yourself and is something you refer back to later to see if you have changed in either column. It is also a way of restoring confidence in yourself and taking a good honest look at yourself and other people.

To close the celebration we did a love circle, which is quite an experience. Everyone stands in a circle. Each member has a turn at standing in the middle of the circle. One by one, members go into the circle and greet that person in any non-verbal way. It sounds easy, but it's really risky when it comes to doing it. People are reluctant at first. It takes a lot of guts to walk out into the middle, and once you get there you get the feeling no one is going to greet you. But everything goes fine and you come out of it with a really great feeling.

For the rest of the time we had a clean-up, lunch and a quick evaluation of what we thought about the weekend. We loaded the cars up and headed home. As with all weekends, going home, back to civilization, and school, and leaving this fantastic environment, was a real kick in the teeth.

Programme 7

Work camp

Picture yourself on this unusual weekend. You're wearing the grubbiest clothes you own. Standing near the top of an 8-foot ladder, hammering plywood to ceiling joists, your hair loses that straight-from-the-stylist look. Beads of perspiration ski down your forehead and somersault off your nose.

Instead of listening to a superstar speaker tell how God can work through your life, you learn at first hand what it's like to rely on God to help you do things you thought you could never do – like working in the cold rain, doing carpentry or plumbing.

In addition to coming home with nostalgic memories and snapshots, you'll be leaving behind rock-solid, see-what-you've achieved results. This weekend will go on helping people long after you've filed your snapshots in a drawer.

Work trekking?

Work trekking is a project using a group of young people from a church who decide to minister to people directly by freely giving their labour and love.

The idea of getting a bunch of friends together for painting projects and minor construction tasks isn't exactly new, but work-trekking takes the group project idea and adds a few unique wrinkles of its own. For instance:

- You discover a needy and worthy project that generally is more then 10 miles from your church, but not more than 50 miles away.
- It is a gift to the people who are the focus of the trek. The food, help, materials, lodging, even the soft drinks are provided by the church.
- It generally combines a youth group project with the entire church helping in the planning and in raising the needed cash.
- Young people do all the carpentry, plumbing, electrical and

masonry work – with skilled adults providing supervision.
- It usually lasts one weekend, and at the most, one week.
- It is designed so work trekkers can return to the site for ministry-type follow-up experiences.

Okay, so you're sold on the work trekking concept. Your church leaders sound interested and your muscles are tingling from the thought of a new challenge.

Find the project that's right for you

Finding a project that's within 50 miles of your church will minimize transport costs, make preparation visits possible, and above all, allow a relationship for future ministries to develop.

In your search for potential projects, check for church facilities needing repair. Also check with local government agencies for elderly or low-income people whose homes need repair. Many of the small people-helping organizations in your area may need a helping hand themselves.

Ask the local newspaper to publicize your search for projects. This stage of the planning process may take several months before you find just the right project for your group.

Factors to consider in choosing a work project: can your church afford the needed materials? Do you have the youth power and the skilled adult help to complete the trek? Are there adequate facilities near the work site to house and feed all the trekkers?

The introduction visit

Once you've found what seems to be the right project, grab your leaders, catering volunteers, construction experts and spend some time at the site. Don't forget to invite interested parents and any adults who want to come along. The earlier you can help the people in your church catch the vision of this special work trekking project, the better.

After getting acquainted and sharing the work trek concept with the people at the work trek site, carefully evaluate the work that needs to be done. Start getting a mental picture of the necessary supplies. You'll also need to make arrangements for sleeping space, toilet facilities, kitchen equipment, a place to eat, a meeting room and transport.

Spend most of your time evaluating potential work trek sites. List every possible project: the jobs to be done, materials needed and number of workers required. A simple diagram of the work sites will help potential workers visualize the work to be done. Discuss the best possible weekend dates with the hosts.

Publicity
Communicate the work trek vision to the entire church as early as you can. Announcements in the church magazine, newsletters and on-the-spot announcements in church services are a must. General interest articles can be written and mailed to everyone in the church.

As details of the work trek start taking shape, share them with the church staff. Plan an entire church service to share the work trek concept.

Since the work trek scene is relatively close, a publicity team can make a special trip to take photos for posters and bulletin boards. A video could tell the whole story visually. Prepare a detailed mailing for everyone who's expressed an interest in the project – trekkers, skilled adults, parents, interested church members, friends. Include in the mailing a covering letter explaining the trek purpose, work site options, plan of work trek activities, dates, what to bring and a challenge for personal ministry.

Local newspapers will generally be happy to run short articles on your plans, especially if you provide good quality black-and-white photos.

Skilled help
Challenge all adults in your church to attend the work trek. But zero in on the trade-skilled people. Get your minister to help you track down those special people. Then go to each person personally and share your trek vision.

Organize into teams
Try to keep the teams balanced by age, sex and interest. Be impartial to sex roles. Boys and girls can – and should – work together as equals in work trekking.

It won't be possible to give every person his or her first choice of work sites. Make sure you distribute the team list one week before the trek. Let the trekkers switch teams if they want to. Then two days before the trek, confirm the arrangements.

About a week before the trek, meet with everyone and discuss work sites, tasks and teams. Pray about last-minute difficulties and needs.

Transport materials to the work trek site
On the night before the trek, load the materials. Use a trailer if you don't have a van. Transport the materials to the site and arrange them at the different work areas. Use posters and signs to help guide teams to their proper work areas.

The trek
Begin with prayer. You'll be able to see the fruit of your careful planning and preparation – the excitement level will be high. You've planned for great results – you'll get them. The adult leaders and skilled adults should be servants: encouraging, motivating, trouble-shooting and getting extra tools, snacks, materials.

When teams get tired, they rest. When they want to talk, they talk. After the work periods are over, a closing communion service can be a life-changing experience. Thank God for how specific people touched your life. It's good to name names and pray for blessings for ministries accomplished.

After the trek
Your first response upon returning home will probably be emotional. You'll be shocked at how much love could be generated through working together. The weekend gave meaning to your whole youth group experience.

Your second response may be a sense of anticlimax. Life will be lonely without your friends working close to you.

Your third response may be guilt – "We should be doing this every weekend."

To keep yourself from crashing too badly, tell your church about your experiences and feelings. Meet with other trekkers about a week after the trek to talk about your feelings. Start talking about ideas for other ministries.

Picture yourself tired, worn out and maybe a little deflated. But you're more mature from experiencing God's work through you and your friends. It's worth the sore muscles.

Programme 8

TV or not TV

Most weekend rules include a ban on TV and radio. Here is a weekend, however, in which a TV set is an important part of the programme. *TV or Not TV?* provides a series of experiences which help the participants probe the medium which probably takes up much of their leisure time. The TV world of values and role models will be compared with the Scriptures so that the young person can be better equipped to choose the good of TV and be on guard against the evil. This should be a fun weekend, and yet one for relating the gospel to an important aspect of contemporary life.

Advance preparation

1. All leaders should thoroughly read over this design and select those portions which they decide to use. If possible a committee including several of the youth group members will decide on this.
2. For this weekend arrange to have one or more TV sets. Check with the centre management about TV reception in the area; if the reception is not good enough you will have to pretape all TV excerpts and bring a video recorder with you.
3. Choose and order any appropriate films for this outline.
4. Bring extra Bibles, a flip chart and felt-tip markers, paper and pencils.
5. Prepare and bring copies of the *TV Profile*. This should look like the example on the next page.

Friday evening: The television experience and my time

1. Give a brief overview of the weekend's theme and activities. This should be designed to arouse the group's enthusiasm as well as to give information.
2. Ask: "Do you have any idea how much time you spend watching TV? We're going to try to get a better idea of this.

My TV viewing profile

Time	Sunday	Monday	Tuesday	Wednesday	Thursday	Friday	Saturday
7 a.m.							
8							
9							
10							
11							
12							
1 p.m.							
2							
3							
4							
5							
6							
7							
8							
9							
10							
11							
12							
1–7 a.m.							

Take one of the TV Viewing Profiles now being passed out and fill it in with a small tick for each hour of the day that you watched TV last week. If last week wasn't typical for you, select another week. Then go back and write in the initials of the name of the programme that you watched at each time. If you can't remember, use these TV magazines to help jog your memory." (NOTE: You might want the group to work through this exercise before going on the weekend. If so, one of the leaders can collate the sheets beforehand and now give a summary of the group's TV profile.)

3. "Were you surprised at how much time you spent watching TV? Most people are. Surveys indicate that the typical family watches TV 4 – 8 hours a day. The higher figure is almost always true when there are children in the household. Where do you fall within this range?

"What other activities do you enjoy? Also list other activities about which you have no choice (school, chores)." Give five minutes so that each person can write down his or her list on the Profile sheet. Ask them also to estimate how much time they spend each day or week at the activities. Ask the members to share their lists. Write the activities down on a flip chart. Included will probably be:

Eating	School
Reading	School club/activities
Talking with friends	Chores
Listening to records/radio	Saturday job
Sports activities	Church
Hobbies	Private devotions/Bible study
Sleeping	Community service

"Which of these activities would you rank among your top five favourites? Which takes up the most time? Which do you have any real choice in? This can give you an idea of where your priorities are."

5. "Let's compare the TV experience with some other activities so that we can see what is unique about each. Where and when do you usually watch TV? With whom? How is watching TV different from these activities?"

a. Reading a book. (More private, intimate than TV since the author can include the characters' thoughts; uses your imagination more since words are just clues as to what a person or the setting looks like; more choice, a whole library full, than of TV programmes; novels are more complex and longer than TV stories.)

b. Going to see a film. (You have to go outside the home; pay; more imposing images due to huge size of screen; cinema is completely darkened so that your attention is forced to the front; yet, the audience reaction is important, such as the comments and cheering in some films.)

c. Listening to radio or record player. (You can do other things such as homework; better sound, especially with headphones or the stereo volume up; wide selection of music of your own choice; you imagine the performer or dream up your own images to go with the music.)

d. Going to a concert or play. (You have to order tickets well in advance; go out of the house; the communal aspect is important, especially at a rock concert.)

6. If you have a TV set available, begin by saying something like: "We've been talking about TV for some time now. Let's watch just a few minutes of it to refresh our minds and get us thinking more about it. We're going to flick through the channels to see what's on tonight." Turn the set on and watch whatever is on for a couple of minutes; then do the same thing with the other channels. (Ignore the groans or plea for "just one minute more"!) If reception is poor, play back a few minutes of TV recorded earlier on your video.

7. What types of TV programme are offered? List these on paper or a flip chart:

Adventure/action stories	Sports
Police/detective stories	TV films
Hollywood feature films	Educational shows
Cartoons	Musical variety shows
Game and quiz shows	Chat shows
Situation comedies	Commercials
Live coverage of events	Concerts

News and documentaries   Religious programmes
Mini-series, TV "novels"   Soap operas

Which are you favourite kinds of programme? Which do you think contribute most to your understanding of life and the world? Which are a waste of time?

Saturday morning: youth, TV and role models

OPTION 1

Say something like "We want to take you back a few years to your childhood. Can you remember ever not having TV? What were your favourite shows when you were little?"

Turn on your TV and watch some cartoons. Or play a pre-recorded video tape of one. Some questions for discussion:

- What is the story about? Is the plot typical of the entire series? Does this cartoon look familiar?
- Who are the main characters? What are they like? Are they believable? If they're superheroes, do they have any human weaknesses? Are they all good, never tempted to use their super powers for themselves? Are the villains entirely evil? What do you think the heroes or villains do in their leisure time?
- Is evil always depicted as something "out there", always in the bad guys? What does the programme say is the best way to fight evil? Is any alternative to violence ever suggested? Compare this with Matthew 26.52 or Romans 12.14–21.
- Is the world as simple as this show suggests? Do you think children should grow up watching such shows without talking them over with adults? Did your parents ever watch such shows with you and talk about them?
- What are some other children's shows that are on Saturday mornings? What are they like?
- What do commercials tell children about what is important in life? How do they tell children about what is important in life? How do the ads match the format of the programmes? Will children have to unlearn any of the things which they are taught by TV?

OPTION 2

1. Divide into groups of three or four. Let each of the groups
    pick a male or female TV character. (You could require that
    half of the groups choose a female.) Each small group
    should describe its character: what he or she looks like; how
    the character relates to people, reacts to crises and deals
    with conflicts; what he or she believes in. What does this
    character suggest an ideal man or woman should be like?
    Compare this with the qualities that Jesus suggests will be
    found among his people in Matthew 5.1–13.
2. How do women come across in TV advertising compared
    with men? Who usually has the problem? Who usually
    enters with the solution? Is this really much different from
    the Popeye and Olive Oyl stories?

Saturday afternoon: TV advertising and gospel values
Watch several TV ads or play back five to ten minutes of pre-
recorded spots. Proceed with the questions below.

*   What do the adverts use to capture your attention? (Camera
    techniques, colour, animation, stars, a story, humour, music,
    etc.)
*   What problem is shown? What promise is made to the view-
    ers?
*   List some of the products that you have bought because of
    TV ads. Did the product live up to the ad's claims? Why or
    why not?
*   List the following dreams/values of a flip chart or OHP. Get
    the group to add the products which promise to fulfil each
    dream/need.

Popularity	Self-esteem
Love	Adventure
Health	Sex-appeal
Nutrition	Security
Success	Good times

How many of these dreams/values are Christian values?

In groups of three or four rewrite the Beatitudes (Matthew

5.1–12) as advertisers' values. After 10-15 minutes let each group share its version with the others. Some examples to get you started:

Blessed are the bold ones who wear Next suits, for they shall inherit the best jobs and girls.

Blessed are those who wear designer jeans, for they shall be considered cool and in the know.

Blessed are you when you are persecuted by pain, for aspirin and paracetamol shall deliver you.

Saturday evening:
A closer look at TV formats and the gospel

1. If yours is a large group, let the members sign up on a first-come, first-served basis to discuss one of the following TV programme formats. Keep the groups evenly divided by limiting the number allowed in each group. Two groups could discuss the same topic.

    a. Situation comedies
    b. Adventure films
    c. Sports
    d. Soap operas
    e. Documentaries

2. The assignment for each group is twofold. First talk over the TV format using specific programmes the groups have seen. Below are some suggested questions and ideas for each format. Then each group should work up a sketch using a Bible story or gospel idea/value as it might come across in that format on TV. Some ideas are suggested, but don't let them limit the groups' imagination.

3. Suggestions and ideas for the TV formats:

    a. Situation comedies

        •   Describe the main characters of several popular sitcoms. What are they like? How do they relate to others? In a manipulative way, maybe, or in a caring way?

- Is the humour in the quirkiness of the characters or in the situation? Are we laughing at or with the person? What's the difference?
- Is the plot believable? That is, have you come away saying, "That's happened to me" or "I know someone like that"?
- What are the proper roles of men and women as suggested by the show? What does the show say is important in life?

b. Adventure films

- Describe the characters. What are they like, and how do they relate to others? What does the series say a man or woman should be and do?
- What is the conflict? How is it resolved, with violence or deceit?
- Does the film shed any light on a human/social problem? Does it oversimplify it or suggest an easy answer?
- Is the hero the kind of person you want to become or have for a friend? How would he or she fit in with Jesus' disciples?

Possible story ideas: rewrite the story of David and Goliath as an episode from a current popular adventure series. Other good stories: the parable of the Good Samaritan and the parable of the Prodigal Son.

c. Sports

- What is the chief aim or point of the sport? What skills do the players need? How much co-operation is needed between them?
- How much does violence or the threat of injury add to the public's interest in the game? In football? Hockey? Formula One racing? Do the cameras and announcers frequently go back to recap a particularly violent moment? Why?
- How important is winning to your enjoyment of the game? How do we regard losers? How was the cross

a sign of losing in the Roman Empire? Was Jesus a winner or a loser according to Roman and Jewish standards? And to those of our own culture?

Develop a game with a cricket format for the other groups to play. Make up questions based on the Bible for the "bowler" to bowl at those "batting". A wrong answer or two consecutive "passes" count as a wicket, and so on. One member of your group serves as "bowler", a couple of others can serve as commentators and make comments on the performance and reputation of the various players. Wait till the end to announce that the winners, in true Christian spirit, will act as waiters at the next meal or perform some other service for the others!

d. Soap operas

- Are all soap operas on in the daytime?
- What makes a soap opera different from a regular drama? (Over-emphasis upon suffering and conniving, a pessimistic viewpoint?)
- Describe some of the characters in popular soap operas. What are they like? How do they relate to others?
- Are the plots and solutions believable?

Some story possibilities: Adam and Eve (see Genesis 2, 3 and 4); David and Bathsheba or the story of Ruth. What elements in the Bible would have to be exaggerated to fit the soap opera format? And left out?
Schedule a time for each group to share its masterpiece, perhaps late in the evening or during the next session. If you can, videotape the sketches, and show them to the group and back home to others too!

Sunday morning

1. Start with a catch-up time for groups who didn't finish everything during a previous session.
2. Help the group summarize what has been learnt.

Some summary questions:

- What are some good points about TV?
- What are some problems or bad points about it?
- How can we use TV as responsible Christians?

WORSHIP/CELEBRATION

- Call to worship – Read Isaiah 55.1 (could be read responsively).

- Hymn of praise.

- Call to confession – Isaiah 55.2. Write a confession based on our too-casual acceptance of TV's false values.

- Assurance of God's pardon – Isaiah 55.3 and John 3.16.

- A song of thanksgiving in response.

- The Scriptures – could be some passages from the earlier sessions.

- Meditation – leader's comments on interaction with the congregation on TV and Isaiah 55.1–3, or TV values and the Beatitudes.

- Closing hymn of commitment.

Programme 9

An all-night lock-in

For a great change of pace, why not try an all-night lock-in? Your young people will get to know each other in ways they never realized. This dusk-to-dawn extravaganza mixes games, foolishness, Bible study, discussion – well, almost anything you want to plan. If planned well, a lock-in can become a high point of your youth programme. Whether you plan a mixture of serious and fun times or whether you plan to skate all night, several basic techniques can increase your lock-in's effectiveness.

The purpose of your all-night event, the planning and the preparation will all affect the lock-in's performance. An all-night lock-in involves the total person on the physical, mental, emotional, social and spiritual levels. Everything that happens affects someone on one of those levels.

Because the lock-in is a time of total involvement it becomes a time of high risk of failure by the youth group. Stress, fatigue and social factors affect activities that would be successful in a normal two-day weekend or a daytime mini-event. These different factors will not necessarily cause a good programme to fail, but they may produce a lack of motivation to get involved in an activity which seems much less exciting at 5 a.m. than at midnight.

Why risk the failure? Because the chance for success is equally high. Fatigue does wonders in lowering a person's personality defences (not to mention a clique's defence mechanisms). Young people who are just "speaking friends" will build a bond of friendship after twelve hours of shoulder-to-shoulder, eye-to-eye contact.

There is an old saying that you should not marry a person until you have seen your prospective spouse with a bad cold or sick with the flu. There is a "knowing" and "being known" that comes out of being dog-tired. Discussions and openness take on

new dimensions when the "make-up" begins to wear off and
superficial techniques wear out.

The following tips can help you increase the potential for
success.

Tips for planning

Begin planning well in advance of a likely date for a lock-in.
Two or three months are usually required. You will need to
meet with different committees three or four times to check up
on how programmes and preparations are progressing. The
committees must have their different programmes clearly in
mind by the last planning session. There are no exceptions. Plan
well and plan in detail if you want a successful lock-in.

Determine the purpose first

It may not be easy to get the entire group to discuss and determine why you want to have a lock-in. Some will want the
overnighter because it was done before or because another
group had one. The "Why are we doing this?" should be clear
to everybody before any lock-in plans are made. The time
you've spent in answering this question will bear fruit at the
lock-in when someone asks, "What are we supposed to be
doing here anyway?"

Drafting a statement of purpose may seem unnecessarily
time-consuming, but it will bring into focus much of what you
plan to do and how it is to be done.

If one goal for your lock-in is to attract other teenagers to
your youth group, you will want to advertise. If you want to
experience and develop a small intimate fellowship, do no
advertising except to let the parents and church leaders know
your plans.

Seven important planning areas

1. RECREATION

Energetic and action-packed recreation times can provide a positive contribution to your lock-in. Determine who will be in
charge of the recreation and sport times. Ask the planning team
to develop a programme the planning committee can discuss.
The key is to have a well-prepared outline of games, sketches

and strenuous physical sports. Explanations of how to play new games should be thought out and any materials needed for the recreation time should be secured well in advance. Have all the things you need at the lock-in site a day early.

Balance recreation time with worship and spiritual programmes. Balance new games with old favourites everybody knows how to play. Balance competitive games with non-competitive games. Balance skill games with non-skill games.

Use physical activity to stimulate and create energy in the early morning hours. Use table games, crafts and songs to fill free time or to make transition to other programmes on the agenda.

How about free time? It is better not to fill up the final hours of your lock-in with free time. If the group is tired the free time may be seen as a signal that the lock-in is over. Getting a final wrap-up session started may be impossible if the group have been dozing for an hour or more.

2. FOOD

Plan food times to follow recreation times or preceding, during and after any film you wish to show. Choose a food committee to prepare, serve and clean up after snack times. Be sure that whatever you plan to serve can be prepared in large quantities with the available facilities. A household oven will keep a lot of burgers or pancakes warm but it will not cook seven pizzas at once. Make arrangements so that you can serve everyone at one go.

3. DEVOTIONS, SPIRITUAL GROWTH AND WORSHIP

Decide if the adult helpers or members of the youth group will be in charge of these sessions. The atmosphere of the room sometimes plays a part in sensitive spiritual times. Setting the stage for a serious spiritual time is especially important if you have been running relays in the area you now plan to worship in.

Balance spiritual times with social and physical sports times. Sunrise devotions seem like a natural but they may be hard to pull off effectively at the end of a lock-in. Physical fatigue becomes a competitive factor to spiritual sensitivity in the early morning hours. The peak spiritual time should come three or four hours in the lock-in while the mind is fresh and the emotions are still responsive.

Choose the music in advance. If you use a guitar be sure the guitarist can play the songs before the song leader teaches them to the group.

4. BIBLE STUDIES OR TRAINING PROGRAMMES

If your lock-in has a theme and you plan three or four sessions around that theme, you can separate each serious session with recreation, food, free time or a film. If free time precedes a serious session, be sure everyone is clear about when and where they are to meet next.

It is difficult to do serious, concentrated thinking much after 3 a.m. Plan to meet your major objectives before that time. Be creative in your teaching method and use a variety of methods to stimulate interest. If small group discussions are planned, break down into small groups by age so that the older people will not dominate their group's discussions. If your youth group is large enough and you have qualified leadership, you can offer optional activities during your lock-in and allow people to choose the one that appeals to them the most.

Place a guest speaker on the programme early and allow him or her to leave during a later session.

5. DISCIPLINE

It is impossible to come up with a set of rules that would cover every possible circumstance. It is best to keep the rules few and simple. Be specific in advertising and in pre-lock-in sessions about appropriate dress at the lock-in. Electronic games, radios, comic books and TVs are not a problem at a marathon rocking session, but strict controls should be placed on them at lock-ins where group and individual participation is crucial to the lock-in's success.

Telephone use should be restricted. Young people should expect to stay for the entire lock-in when they come. Check with parents if a teenager needs to leave early.

6. FINANCES

Mention the cost in every lock-in advertisement. Plan how and when to collect money so that no one fails to pay. It is a good idea to close registration two or three days before the lock-in so that final food plans and financial arrangements can be made. If possible, collect all monies before the lock-in. This gives them an added incentive to come to the event even though some other activity may come up at the last minute.

7. STARTING WITH A BANG

What happens during the first hour sets the tone for the entire lock-in. Plan the first hour to involve everybody. Arrange surprises to excite them about the rest of the lock-in.

Four things need to happen at the beginning of the lock-in:

- Reduce tension and nervousness while building a sense of community. This can be done in many ways but usually involves doing strange and unusual things together such as crazy songs, unusual exercises or weird games.
- Get in touch with the overall group feelings, attitudes and expectations about the lock-in. Simple, non-threatening questions allow people to express something about their current emotional state. (Such as: "The colour I most feel like..." or "The things I hope to get out of this lock-in are...").
- Clarify rules, purpose and timetable. Answer questions about the rules and timetable.
- Determine teams for relay and sports events to break down existing cliques and contribute to the overall unity of the youth group. Random drawing or fun exercises help the young person identify with and belong to his or her new team. Controlling the team formations reinforces the similarities among the members in the group and allows them to discover important things about other members.

With your purpose clearly in mind and a well-planned, well-prepared programme your youth group can create lifetime memories – and short-term fatigue – at your most successful lock-in.

Selected reading list

GENERAL GUIDANCE

The Complete Youth Manual, Vols 1 & 2 by Steve Chalke: Kingsway

Christian Youth Work by Mark Ashton: Kingsway

Working with Teenagers by Nick Aiken: Marshall Pickering

Tension Getters by Mike Yaconelli and David Lynn: Bible Society

Just Looking by John Allan: Bible Society

PRACTICAL IDEAS

Power Lines by Bob Moffett: Scripture Union

Power Pack, Vols 1 & 2 by Bob Moffett: Scripture Union

Crowdbreakers (games and activities) by Bob Moffett: Marshall Pickering

Crowdmakers (ideas and lessons) by Bob Moffett: Marshall Pickering

Youthbuilders by N Aiken and P Angier: Marshall Pickering

A selection of helpful organizations and agencies for resources or information

Action Centres UK, Hereward Wake House, Gladstone Road, Northampton NN5 7EG

Bagster Video, Westbrook House, 76 High Street, Alton, Hants GU34 1EN

Baptist Union Youth Office, 4 Southampton Row, London WC1B 4AB

Bible Society, Stonehill Green, Westlea, Swindon SN5 7DG

Catholic Fund for Overseas Development (CAFOD), 2 Romero Close, Stockwell Road, London SW9 9TY

Catholic Youth Services, 41 Cromwell Road, London SW7 2DH

Christian Aid, Partnership House, 157 Waterloo Road, London SE1 8XA

Christian Video Library, The Hub Christian Resources Centre, 162 Greenford Road, Harrow, Middlesex HA1 3QS

Church of England: Board of Education, Church House, Dean's Yard, London SW1P 3NZ

Church Pastoral Aid Society (CYPECS), Falcon Court, 32 Fleet Street, London EC4Y 1DB

Church Missionary Society, Partnership House, 157 Waterloo Road, London SE1 8UU

Frontier Youth Trust, 130 City Road, London EC1V 2NJ

Methodist Association of Youth Clubs, 2 Chester House, Pages Lane, Muswell Hill, London N10 1PR

Scripture Union, 130 City Road, London EC1V 2NJ

United Society for the Propagation of the Gospel (USPG), Partnership House, 157 Waterloo Road, London SE1 8XA

Video-Aid, Mill House, 23 Mill Road, Worthing, West Sussex BN11 4LD